IT TAKES A
CHURCH WITHIN
A VILLAGE

IT TAKES A CHURCH WITHIN A VILLAGE

H. B. London, Jr.
and
Neil B. Wiseman

THOMAS NELSON PUBLISHERS
Nashville • Atlanta • London • Vancouver

Published in Nashville, Tennessee, by Thomas Nelson, Inc., Publishers, and distributed in Canada by Word Communications, Ltd., Richmond, British Columbia.

The Bible version used in this publication is THE NEW KING JAMES VERSION. Copyright © 1979, 1980, 1982, Thomas Nelson, Inc., Publishers.

ISBN 0-7852-7211-9

Printed in the United States of America

1 2 3 4 5 6 — 01 00 99 98 97 96

Dedicated
to Children Everywhere

especially

William Wiseman
7

Taylor London
6

Hilary London
5

Amanda London
5

Katie Wiseman
2

Jeffrey London
1 month

CONTENTS

Part 3: Architects of the Enduring

THE CHILDREN MUST HAVE YOUR HELP

Do you hear the children crying? The evening news brings harmed, neglected, abandoned flesh-and-blood children into our living rooms every day. The situation is bad and getting worse. Children are hurting—and hurting badly. Meanwhile, politicians are unable or unwilling to do anything to ease the pain. Unless someone intervenes, we can expect children to repeat their parents' patterns in the next generation because that's all they know.

Children wait for people like us to transform situations they didn't cause and don't understand. We can no longer tolerate a permissive society that shortchanges millions of boys and girls. As members of the greatest unheard minority in the world, children are forced to grow up too quickly because innocence has been strangled out of childhood. Something has to be done now.

The song advises, "Teach your children well." But how—when values crumble, violence increases, crime multiplies, and culture appears bent on ruining the future of children? Who knows how to teach them well? Children of our land need mighty miracles, not the kind that drop out of heaven, but the warm, fuzzy, spendthrift kind created by people who love them most. So, what can you do, and will you do it?

The message of this book is simple but amazingly profound. Government is unable to fix our children's problems, but we can. The starting point is to love every child into greatness and to help every child develop his or her full potential. This book challenges the church and the family to reclaim their influence on children and their environments. Though we believe it takes something like a village to save a child, we know the church and the family are probably the only institutions that even faintly resemble a village in our time. That fact gives every church amazing obligations and abundant opportunities. We must meet obligation and opportunity with competence and gusto.

This book issues four pressing calls to action:

- A call to empower and resource strong marriages and stable families, so they may become even stronger.
- A call to spiritually and emotionally adopt children whose families are broken or dysfunctional.
- A call to improve ministry to families in every possible way.
- A call to strengthen everyone spiritually regardless of family status, so the strengths spill over into families.

Everyone in our society has some interest in the well-being of the next generation. Therefore, we must get beyond assigning blame to loving kids one at a time until we precipitate a transforming revolution.

We, the authors of this book, want to see more loving care for children provided. We are not interested in more theories. All the abstractions and conceptualizations about children in our society remind us of a reported conversation between Dean Rusk, former secretary of state, and a woman at a dinner party. When asked about foreign affairs, Mr. Rusk gave a long explanation. Then the woman replied, "Thank you so much. I now am at a higher level of confusion than I have ever been before." The children in our land do not need a higher level of confusion or more dialogue or additional task forces. They need loving action. Children everywhere need more love from more people.

Someone has suggested with hope that all the problems we face may be the birth pangs of the next great awakening. Pray God that such an awakening is on its way and that He will start the awakening through our service to boys and girls.

This book is for everyone who loves children. It's for everyone who wants children to have better lives. Read on about what needs to be done and what can be done. See all children who come into your life through the eyes of Jesus—they are precious in His sight.

ACKNOWLEDGMENTS

Thanks to Dr. Miriam Hall, lover of children; experienced public, Sunday school, and seminary teacher; loyal churchwoman; and longtime friend of the Wisemans for helping us develop ideas and opening her heart and files to us.

Thanks to Victor Oliver for proposing the book's idea and for believing the project could be completed in record time.

Thanks to Sue McFadden for amazing follow-through.

Thanks to Bonnie Wiseman for making the copy come out right through four rewrites.

Thanks to Brian Hampton for making the sentences readable and interesting.

Thanks to the Thomas Nelson publishing team—though we have not met many of you, we know this book could not have been published without your artistry and skills.

Thanks to our spouses, colleagues, and students for stories and ideas.

Thanks to authors, columnists, and writers for allowing us to quote you and your stories.

It Takes a
Church Within
a Village

PART 1
CHILDREN—A GENERATION IN CRISIS

Chapter 1

THANKS, MRS. CLINTON

A Wake-Up Call to Save Our Children

We want to thank Mrs. Clinton—for her book, *It Takes a Village*. We applaud her call to value children more and to put them at the top of our nation's priorities. The country desperately needs her reminder—our most precious resource is our children. They deserve to be the object of our love, our resources, and our commitments because they are our priceless possession for today and our hope for tomorrow. In our heart of hearts, we know that a nation cannot neglect its children without squandering its present and jeopardizing its future. Children make up the families, communities, churches, and culture of our future.

As we read her book, we felt curiosity, sometimes fascination, and often grief. We identified with the sorrow and pain. Often her use of the word *village* seemed too diffused for solving such a big problem—something like a bucket of water to put out a forest fire. We wondered how villages can save our children when so much that resembles a village seems to be disappearing so rapidly in North America.

Thanks for Warning Us

Mrs. Clinton's challenge to move children up to a higher level of significance needs to be heard and heeded, from the coast of Maine to the beaches of California and from the mouth of the Columbia River in Oregon and Washington to the farthest tip of the Florida Keys. She accurately warns us, "Even though our national rhetoric proclaims that children are our most important resource, we squander these precious lives as though they do not matter."[1] After all is said and done, more is said than done.

We thank her for reminding us that children's problems are among the toughest issues we face. We thank her for helping us realize that children can't speak up for themselves in the same way as other special interest groups so often do. She is right to call us to face the fact that children "are intimately connected to the very essence of who we are and who we will become."[2] As she explains carefully and thoughtfully, our children are a precious national resource for the future, but they are also valuable for who they are now. They carry the nation's future in their potential, but they are also an integral part of the nation's present.

Thanks for Stretching Our Awareness

We thank Mrs. Clinton for calling everyone to attention and action. It's so easy to think the problem belongs to someone else. She reminds us that while all people are not parents or grandparents, we all have firsthand knowledge of what it means to be a kid because each of us was one once. We thank her for convincing us that all of us—parents and even people without children—have a serious stake in seeing that children are cherished and that we must be sure they get a better break in the future than they are getting now.

Since reading her book, we have become more aware of children around us. We watched a young colleague relate to his children, ages two and seven, at Wendy's. He is a wonderful father, and his children will become whole adults. We made friends with children, ages four and nine, on a plane trip to New York. They shared their candy bars with us—it was their idea, and we loved it. We met a couple as they brought their one-week-old son to church for the first time. And Sunday's paper in St. Louis ran a story about a couple, soon to celebrate their fiftieth wedding anniversary, who raised six children of their own and provided foster care to seventy other children. Great kids and hurting kids are around us everywhere.

Thanks for Reminding Us Children Can't Wait

The faces of hundreds of children we have known came to mind as we read Mrs. Clinton's book. She made us remember that children keep being born, keep growing up, and keep making choices that affect their lives forever. She made us realize that kids don't wait for Congress or clergy or parents to decide what needs to be done. Children grow up while government, school districts, and social scientists argue whether society can afford much-needed, though costly, reforms. Boys and girls can't wait for us to show at-risk parents life skills for helping their children develop. Children don't wait. They can't.

Her statistics are frightening. In one paragraph, she reports that "one in five children in America live in poverty; ten million children do not have private or public health care coverage; homicide and suicide kill almost seven thousand children every year; one in four of all children are born to unmarried mothers, many of whom are children themselves; and 135,000 children bring guns to school each day."[3] Children from every stratum of society suffer from abuse, neglect, and solvable emotional problems. The numbers stun us even more when we remember they represent individuals who might change the world or invent the cure for cancer or take Billy Graham's place in the next generation. What a horrible waste!

We were moved to courageous action when Mrs. Clinton told her readers that people cannot roll up their sleeves and get to work while wringing their hands. That's why we wrote this book.

Could the Church Be Our Brightest Hope?

While reading Mrs. Clinton's book, we wished she had said a lot more about the church. More about its effectiveness. More about its potential for character development. More about shaping our society. More about every family needing a church more now than ever before to help them raise children in our fragmented society. We wanted her and others to believe the church, even with its weaknesses, is our only hope for developing and cherishing well-adjusted children. The church may be the only nearby village that has even a remote possibility of giving children what they really need. And the church, unlike other institutions, can respond immediately.

We appreciated Mrs. Clinton's references to the influences of the Methodist church in her life and the Baptist church in the life of the president. Several sentences seemed to imply that churches helped them live nice, respectable lives—something like learning to be pleasant to one's neighbor or learning to stop pushing other kids on the play-ground. Maybe we were too suspicious, or perhaps we missed the intent, but in her book the discussion of the church sounded like more of the too-prevalent American notion that the church is good, but we must be careful not to get too much of such a good thing. The popular notion is to exercise cautious moderation in relationship to Christ and His cause. Meanwhile the New Testament calls the people of God to become radically involved in a community of faith that transforms all who participate and, at the same time, salts a society with righteousness.

Please Expect More of the Church

The problem—*It Takes a Village* expects too little of the church. While Mrs. Clinton calls America to establish more tight-knit, trusted, nurturing relationships with children, most social agencies and entities of our society are moving away from the child.

Therefore, the church must be called and challenged and charged with filling this vacuum. Think of the isolation children experience when they wait two hours every afternoon in a locked house until their parents come home from work. Think of the isolation children feel when neighbors do not know their names and of their fear when classmates carry guns to school. Think what children miss when extended families live hundreds of miles away. The list goes on and on. In such an environment, the church needs local and national leaders to push and pull Christians into being what God made the family at church to be.

Please Take the Church Seriously

This too-common inside and outside view, as we have said, is that church probably won't harm you if you don't take it too seriously. This reasoning says the church is usually positive, but be careful not to accept everything you hear there. Like a green apple, a church might make you ill if you eat too much. Or like a rich dessert, it might clog your arteries or make you mentally obese.

A woman's voice on the church phone one Sunday morning about eight o'clock stated, "I'd like to come this morning, Reverend, but I don't know what time the performance starts."

Another said, "I'd like to drop by and catch the service today if I can find time."

And an usher, well into his eighties and given to speaking too loudly because of his hearing loss, said in a stage whisper to a visitor during the benediction, "Don't worry about all this rugged preaching. Our young pastor sometimes gets carried away about how we are supposed to live."

America doesn't take the church seriously enough. Nor does the church take itself seriously enough. Both of these realities have to be corrected if our children are to be placed at the top of our combined agendas.

Please Cherish the Church's Potential Impact

All of this caution is strange talk when God intends the church to be the family of God. Lots of family words are used in church, such as *brothers* and *sisters, community of faith, family I never had,* or *my adopted spiritual family.* The church is a two-thousand-year continuance of a group of followers Jesus called His family when they did the will of God (Matt. 12:50). Try this logic. In family relationships, does anyone ever advise another not to get too close to her kin? Do we ever tell a child not to love his parents too much? Does anyone ever advise a young couple not to become too emotionally involved in their marriage? Cautions about the church make about as much sense.

This notion of not depending on the close relationships at church to heip raise a child sounds irrational and self-defeating at a time when Americans appear to want to connect more but don't know how. This fear of wholeheartedness toward God should frustrate us when we know deep down that authentic relationships are as essential to our inner health as the air we breathe is essential to our physical health. All of this sounds confusing in a world that is hungry for the love of God but doesn't know what it is, even as it is dying to experience the fulfilled life that Christ so generously promises.

Let's Take the Church Public

Our closely guarded privacies can become our prisons. With faxes, E-mail, phones, TVs, and computers, we can know nearly everything without knowing anyone. Millions are lonely in a crowd and do not know what to do about it. Meanwhile, the church—at its best a place of meaning and belonging—is often ignored because so few have even considered its potential to truly become a village of faith for children and for their parents.

Consider the Possibilities

The church may be among our best hopes for reaping the values of a village and creating a meaningful sense of community. Like nothing else, the church can be the family we don't have and a community that loves us even when we are not as lovable as we ought to be. God intends the church to be a reservoir of acceptance, a community of courage, a source of wisdom, a group that demands accountability, a pattern of righteousness, and a stimulation for faith. Lately, we have been thinking about what could happen if every congregation truly became such a church—a resource center where human beings find new lives for old, where they receive peace in place of fragmentation, where they find forgiveness of sin, where they are provided freedom from loneliness, and where they find healing for brokenness.

The church in nearly every setting can provide the needed sense of belonging. Such a sense of belonging results from an authentic, attractive blending of who Christ really is to us personally with caring and compassion and cooperation and community that develops character.

Let's Do It

The challenge calls every Christian to remold churches into development centers that are energized by the incredible promises of Christ and the empowerment He provides. That means putting a higher priority on children. That means teaching boys and girls that Christ is a genuine Friend of all children. In this refocusing process, we will rediscover a long-forgotten but amazing force in the community of faith to energize our adoptive family relationships. This effort will open our hearts as it stretches our spirits. It will question our timidity and shyness so that we might really get to know one another and not be afraid to trust or to give and receive love again. Or it might even be the first time for those who have never experienced these benefits in churches they attend.

Then we will love the church for our children's sake. Our love will strengthen the church for our boys and girls. As we nourish our children in such a community of faith, we will be made whole and holy ourselves. The caring climate of the church will be a magnet of grace and a living example of Jesus' words, "By this all will know that you are My disciples, if you have love for one another" (John 13:35). Thousands of such rekindled churches could transform the plight of children. It needs to be done, and it can be done. Therefore, it must be done.

Admit Society Can't Do It Without a Strengthened Church

The pressing question in a confused society that is wasting its children is, Can anyone raise a child to emotional well-being and spiritual wholeness without the family of God? Though it may be possible, it is not likely.

Is there not a spiritual quest at the center of every unsatisfied self? Is not the search for meaning precisely what is so desperately missing in what we so often now teach our children? To ignore the spiritual dimension of human development is to deny a significant part of being human that will not go away. And that is what we are doing when we have second- and third-generation parents trying to raise children who have no memory of the church or no experience of God.

The second question may be the flip side of the first: Can the church responsibly continue to fiddle with nonessentials while the needs of millions of contemporary children are not being met? Or to say it another way, Can the church be satisfied to live out the nursery rhyme of the cat who went to London to see the queen but settled for seeing the mouse under the queen's chair?

Too often, the church is accused of being irrelevant because that's what the church has allowed itself to become in too many places. If you are not convinced, listen to the agendas in local, area, and denominational meetings of the church. It's time for every church and every church agency to get back in the race and win. Our times demand it.

Since the church can do better, it must do better. The church has more to offer children than anyone can imagine. Even where the family of God is weak, can't we prescribe treatment or surgery to help it become vigorous and healthy? Wouldn't that be easier than starting all over to remake a village where nobody knows your name and lots of people have moved to the big city?

Consider All the Nearby Branch Offices

Little towns are dying; schools bus kids out of their environments; some public school teachers have become bone weary or overprofessionalized; and neighborhoods in Manhattan and Miami have been turned into armed camps controlled by gangs. But the church has outposts on Main Street in every community, town, and city where Mario, Mary, Tom, Fatma, and Nick can be called by their first names and where they can hear the stories of Jesus. When the church responds to such a significant need, we will all be strengthened—the children strengthened, the family strengthened, the father strengthened, the mother strengthened, the grandfather strengthened, and the grandmother strengthened. We need that now. And since the church is still located on so many Main Streets, let's refocus its mission, renew its commitment, and revitalize its impact. Unlike any other institution or agency, the church is uniquely located near the problem and can become supernaturally empowered to nurture the moral and spiritual development of children.

Learn from Community Programs

Although *Washington Post* editorials seldom provide high moments of spiritual guidance, one of William Raspberry's columns moved us more than a sermon by a fiery evangelist could. In his editorial "Rediscovering the Power of the Spirit," Raspberry told about Robert Woodson's work as the founder and president of the National Center for Neighborhood Enterprise in Washington who reported,

> For twenty years people, including me, would check out the successful social programs—I'm talking about the neighborhood-based healers who manage to turn people around—and we would report on such things as size, funding, facilities or technique. Only recently has it crystallized for me that the one thing virtually all these successful programs had in common was a leader with a strong sense of spirituality. . . . I'm not saying that spiritually based programs always work, only that the successful programs almost always have a spiritual base.[4]

When Raspberry questioned Woodson about the implications of these insights for national social service policies, Woodson answered, "I'm not sure I know yet. But I do know that the hunger I sense in America is not a hunger for things but a search for meaning. We don't yet have scales to weigh the ability some people have to supply meaning, to provide the spiritual element I'm talking about."[5] That spiritual element is what makes every church a potentially viable village for children. Review that incredibly insightful summary again: "I'm not saying that spiritually based programs always work, only that the successful programs almost always have a spiritual base." What implications that conclusion has for the church!

Take Your Pick—Ships, Remedies, or Communities of Grace

Perhaps we should use medical metaphors to be sure the church is actually involved in many phases of spiritual and emotional wellness, including prenatal care, prevention, nutrition, mental health, healing, surgery, and geriatrics. Everyone benefits when the church becomes a healing village of God's grace where emotional health and spiritual wholeness can be found. Even when it can't be found anywhere else, the church can be the place where a child feels safe, cherished, and nurtured—a developmental place where everyone who influences the child in any way is loved by the child as part of an adopted family. Though that impact on the child may be hard to accomplish in a society where so many worship themselves, it is what our children need most and an effective way to rejuvenate the church at the same time. So let's make it happen.

Whenever we think the captains of the church should do something about the disabled ship called the church, about to be swamped in so many places, let's remember we are really the captains of our churches.

In the last several paragraphs, we have given you a variety of metaphors—ships, medical remedies, and grace villages. Take your pick, but do something to transform the church's ministry where you are.

The Village of God Must Accept the Challenge

A Jewish lullaby sings about a river where something deep within us runs out of what has been, what we now are, and what is to be transmitted to the next generation. That's precisely what the church has to do in every era, especially ours. The village of God has to communicate what has been, what is, and what is to come:

1. What has been, the history of God's faithfulness since creation until now.
2. What God is doing in us, and it is marvelous.
3. And what all of this means to the next generation, our children.

To put it more succinctly, the church must nurture all children to faith, become an adoptive family for those who have no family, and empower existing families to nourish faith.

To think of applying the Christian faith to all three of these dimensions at the same time, let's return to several strong ideas from Mrs. Clinton's book where a church can become like the village she proposes.

Make Your Church an Extended Adopted Family

In the book *It Takes a Village,* the term *village* is taken from an African proverb; village means a place and a relationship where many neighbors and members of an extended family feel responsible for one another and all the children. Everybody knows everybody, and everyone has everyone else's best interests at heart.

As the book explains, the essence of the village is a "network of values and relationships that support and affect our lives." That's a beautiful description of what the church as the family of God is on its best days. The First Lady does the church a favor with her definition and her call for a village. Upon hearing Mrs. Clinton's challenge, churches must rethink their impact on children and the effectiveness of their ministries to children and their families. The church's task is to provide a network of relationships to share and shape values—values given us by the living Christ.

Now is a critical time to ask, Do the children of our congregation and community think of the church as a place where they belong like a member of an extended family? Is the church really central to their lives? Surely, the church is more essential to a child's well-being than civic activities, Scout troops, good grades, or music lessons, as important as these things are. Reexamining the work of the village of God takes us back to the reality that this extended family at church is not something to be added to an already busy schedule. Rather, it is the Christ-centering factor in the extended family of God that gives everything else meaning.

Show Children Christ

Admittedly, there is much debate about the size of churches these days. Let's not raise artificial barriers between congregations on the basis of size. In smaller churches, children can be acquainted with everyone in the fellowship; in larger churches, children may be acquainted with just as many people, but not everyone. The question is not size but strength of relationship and a sense of belonging. Ideally, the entire congregation cherishes children. The pastor greets children warmly whenever he or she meets them at church. Sunday school personnel know the children's names. Children should feel that they are key players in the church, much as they might feel at a family reunion of their extended biological families.

A two-hundred-member church in Texas intentionally builds the self-worth of children. Three adults take a special interest in each child by assignment for a full year. The three are a Sunday school teacher, a second adult who contacts the child every week either by mail or by phone, and a third adult friend who prays for the child by name every day. No one should be surprised to learn that this church keeps growing by adding new young families. It's a reality of contemporary life that every couple with children wonder whether they can do the parenting task as well as it needs to be done. It's tough work without the village of God to help.

In this caring-for-children Texas church, every Sunday is a family reunion where every child looks forward to being cherished by at least three adults at church beyond her own family. Adults, whose children are grown and gone, take their special child home to dinner on Sunday, or they go out together to a restaurant. The children of that church are bringing incredible unity to the entire church as the congregation feels the impact of the promise of Scripture: "A little child shall lead them" (Isa. 11:6).

Having been away for about twelve or thirteen years from a church I (Neil) served, I was recently visited by two young men who are now taking leadership roles in that church. We went to lunch, and they talked with maturity about their dreams for the future of their church. They were fourteen when I moved from that church. I can't believe how much they have developed, but much of what they learned in their church's ministry to children and youth about acceptance, forgiveness, tolerance, and love is bearing fruit in their adult years. You can be sure I was proud and grateful for the strong relational ministry that church developed during their teen years.

Renew the Nation

Though history seldom calls them by name, the Christian church in every age has had congregations that thought theirs was the worst of times but decided to flood the darkness with light. Other congregations decided to merely hold on until their translation to glory while they dreamed Christ would return in their lifetimes. They did nothing but allow their country's condition to worsen, leaving a terrible situation for the next generation.

Of course, our times are frustrating. But God is not one bit afraid of this era, and He has providentially placed us in this generation to do what He wants done.

As we read Mrs. Clinton's book, the question kept coming to us like a haunting refrain of an old song, What has the church done to salt and leaven society to solve problems of children in our time? Though no one can be totally unaffected by society's influences, surely, the church can make a difference in children's lives when we consider the power of God, the church's personnel, and the church's mission. This idea kept coming up during the 1996 Promise Keepers for Pastors in Atlanta: What could 40,000 clergy (there are at least 300,000 additional pastors who could not attend) and their congregations do to change the lives of children?

Obviously, no one can take his life or church back to another time or place. But let's face reality. Building an effective village for the care and nurture of children probably can't and won't be done without the church, and why try? The church is close by—a ready-made vehicle for taking up the charge, and every congregation will be mightily strengthened by the exercise.

Consider What Motivates Us

The love of Christ constrains us. Pushes us. Drives us. Compels us. Empowers us to do more for children. Mrs. Clinton reminds us often that helping children is in our own best interest. And she is right. But the love of Christ always calls us to more than self-interest. It motivates us to give ourselves to others' interests. It instructs us to give a cup of cold water because someone is thirsty. To give a coat because someone is cold. To hug because someone needs an affirming touch. And to give because someone needs something we can give.

Christ calls us. Conscience calls us. Our country calls us. Our children call us. Broken families call us. Our commitment calls us. "Straight ahead" is the command of our Champion of children—the Lord God. It is doubtful that the situation of today's children will be significantly changed without the motivating influence of Christ to cause millions to stop talking and start doing. Our society has already tried more money, more social workers, more public housing, more welfare, more education—more and more and more. Yet the problems are still with us that we had at the start, only bigger. Didn't Jesus say to folks who believed religion was to be focused like a laser beam on adults, "Bring those children to Me right now"?

The Village of God Is the Place to Start

We again offer our thanks to Mrs. Clinton for opening a national forum on the subject of improving the lives of children everywhere by a caring society, a generous people, and an aware country. As we see it, the church is the only delivery system for accomplishing such a goal. Though the church may suffer from arthritis and apathy, the problems can be cured by God as this new challenge is accepted.

We find enormous hope in the family of faith—the redeemed people of God who genuinely know they are sons and daughters of God, joint heirs with Jesus, brothers and sisters with the redeemed of all ages. These are the ones God is giving a new vision to change the world through children even as He calls us back to the clear teaching of Scripture—a child shall lead them.

It takes a church at the center of the human village to help a child discover God. It takes a church to lead people to become a Christian change agent for the next generation and beyond. Let's make the family of God viable and interesting and energetic for enriching the spiritual lives of children.

NOTES

1. Hillary Rodham Clinton, *It Takes a Village* (New York: Simon & Schuster, 1996), 16.

2. Ibid.

3. Ibid.

4. William Raspberry, "Rediscovering the Power of the Spirit," as printed in the *Denver Post,* December 1992.

5. Ibid.

Chapter 2

WHO'LL TAME THE JUNGLES?

Check Out the Family of God

Villages turn into a moral jungle when families are sacrificed on the altar of parental selfishness. Villages become sickening swamps when Christian values are sacrificed on the altar of irrelevant drivel and empty traditional forms. We gravely undermine the ability of every kind of village to care for children when we allow our homes to become marital war zones and our churches to become museums of the glorious past. Spiritually strong churches and emotionally healthy homes are society's main defenses against what is happening to today's children.

To give up on the family or the church causes an insidious social and spiritual cancer that destroys our children's innocence even as it weakens their trust and security. The reality: Too many churches have been victimized by the sins of our society and ourselves. Spiritual shallowness and social pathology have been allowed to wound whole congregations. In this self-inflicted wounding and our incredible retrenchments, we gave up too much. Our children have a right to resent our malfeasance of duty, and we don't fully realize the harm we have done to them.

Let me share a riveting experience from a trip to London.

We saw J. B. Priestley's classic play *An Inspector Calls,* which has been playing for about forty years in London's West End. The play opens with a middle-class father, Arthur Birling, telling his grown son, Eric, and his future son-in-law, Gerald Croft, that young men have a right to live in the fast lane where everyone does whatever seems right to him. Then Police Inspector Goole enters, informing the three men of the suicide of a young woman named Eva Smith.

Seeking to build a case, Goole tells them Eva had several aliases, shows her picture to all three men, and asks many probing questions. As the play continues, every character thinks he or she had a part in Eva's death. Arthur Birling was her employer and fired her for participating in a worker-organized strike. Sheila Birling, the daughter, had a selfish fit because she thought Eva, then employed at a dress shop, had laughed at her, so she complained to the shop owner, who fired Eva. In the inspector's questioning, it turns out Gerald had an affair with Eva but broke it off. So Mr. Birling, Sheila, and Gerald feel responsible for the death—all for different reasons. Now enters Sybil Birling, a society matron and mother of Sheila. She heads a social service organization that denied help to Eva because she was pregnant and unmarried, though Sybil did not know that her son, Eric, was the unborn child's father.

For a large part of the play, it appears that Eva was strongly influenced to take her life by the job losses Mr. Birling and Sheila caused, by the rejection of Gerald, by Mrs. Birling's refusal of her request for help, and by the hopelessness caused by Eric's actions. What a mess for one family!

As the London *Evening Standard* reported, "When Inspector Goole arrives to question the Birlings about a young woman's death, it is not long before he discovers the whole family shares responsibility for her suicide. . . . When the Birlings' life is rent asunder, the house actually collapses." All members of the family become victims of their victimizing of others.

It's true about today's children, too. Many leaders of society and parents bear more responsibility than they realize for problems children face. Children are hurt when employers downsize businesses or fire their mom or dad. Children are hurt when compassionate support is withheld. Children are placed at risk by rejection from a thousand different sources. And character never fully develops in children who are shaped solely by secular values. Many persons and many forces in our global village bear responsibility for harming or neglecting a child.

The Moral Jungles Must Be Tamed

Wildernesses and jungles are terribly hard to tame. But it can be done. Think of those rugged pioneers from America's history who pushed back the walls of the wilderness by clearing forests, fording rivers thought uncrossable, climbing mountains thought unclimbable, and risking their lives in so many ways. Or try to imagine an African village in the bush country where natives feared wild beasts and warring neighboring tribes, where they were suspicious of medical treatments, shunned educational opportunities, and were shackled by generations of enslaving superstitions.

On the American frontier and in the African jungle, life was cheap, futures were bleak, and the human spirit was locked into despair. It's not a pretty picture. Think how hard it was to live with imminent danger and impending death.

Though contemporary jungles are in different locations,

children still fear for their lives. Frightening foes still seek to destroy them. Though frontiers no longer exist in the western U.S., our children are locked in human-constructed jungles.

Consider one of the jungles—family breakdown and liberal divorce laws. Dr. Bruce C. Hafen, provost and professor of law at Brigham Young University, delivered a sobering speech at the American Bar Association annual meeting on August 6, 1995, when he said:

> Most of the evidence is incontrovertible, even though competing ideological perspectives on the evidence keep the debate alive. As the ABA Working Group notes, "one in four children in this country is raised by one parent, due in large part to geometric increases in births outside of marriage and in the divorce rate over the last three decades." David Popenoe and Jean Bethke Elshtain estimate that 50 percent of first marriages taking place today are likely to end in divorce. Professor Glendon's comparative studies show that American law has taken the freedom to obtain a divorce further than the law of any Western nation, including Sweden, exhibiting a level of "carelessness" about "the economic casualties of divorce [that is] unique among Western countries." The U.S. also now produces a higher proportion of out-of-wedlock births than any other nation. In 1960, only 5 percent of all births occurred to unmarried mothers. By 1990, nearly a quarter of all U.S. births took place outside marriage.[1]

Hafen later added these consequences to his speech:

> Children in single-parent or step-parent families are more likely than children in intact families to be poor, to drop out of school, to have trouble with the law—to do worse, in short, by most definitions of well being. They are also more

likely to be abused, to have physical and emotional problems, and to abuse drugs. And, contrary to popular assumptions, these children do not always "bounce back" after divorce or remarriage; instead, many of their problems continue. In significant part because of the higher proportion of children in single parent families, a national commission recently concluded, "never before has one generation of American teenagers been less healthy, less cared for, or less prepared for life than their parents were at the same age."[2]

How much worse does the social misery have to get before Christian people take action to model well-adjusted, Christ-fulfilling marriages and to highlight examples of the truly good life? The jungles have to be tamed for the sake of the children, and the time is now.

Children fear for their lives in our moral jungles. Meanwhile, adults fail to spiritually nourish children, or perhaps they have forgotten how to do it, if they ever knew. Children have been moved hundreds of miles from their extended families. Many teachers no longer try to teach children because of their own fears or their lack of preparation—some were given college degrees because they showed up for college classes somewhat regularly. Government on nearly every level from community to school board to state to federal and global provides us with more empty rhetoric and bureaucratic nonsense than nourishment for our children. Yet in these troubling times, many churches are more focused on dealing with significantly less important issues than showing children how to live.

The Jungles Keep Gaining on Us

Parents, many of them teenagers themselves with no parenting models to guide them, use welfare or minimum-wage work to provide designer duds for their children while providing no nourishment for their children's minds or souls. A hospital nurse from a maternity ward lamented after she released an unmarried mother and her beautiful baby, "When they went through these hospital doors, that child left the only peace it is likely to ever know to enter a war game of crime and hate. I wish it were possible to shelter the baby from what he is so likely to face."

Consider carefully what *Los Angeles Times* columnist Suzanne Fields calls the urban rat-packs. She reports,

> We've got a big problem in the United States: Young men in groups. Increasing numbers of boys at ever younger ages are sexually aggressive, violent, vicious. Two girls, 14 and 16, of Houston were raped repeatedly and then strangled with a belt and shoe laces. The suspects, six Houston teen-agers ranging in age from 14 to 18 years old, stomped on the necks of the girls to make sure they were dead.
>
> The atrocities committed by young men under 18 are epidemic, an increase of 85 percent in five years, according to the FBI. All kinds of crimes are on the increase by teen-age rat-packs. Research suggests that 85 percent of juvenile crime takes place in groups.[3]

The columnist continues, "Playground sport now includes a recreational pastime called 'pretending rape.' A 12-year-old girl in Yonkers, New York, told police how eight boys, ages 9 to 13, threw her down on the ground and aggressively fondled her. School officials told the *New York Times* that the boys had been 'playing a rape game' that got out of hand."[4]

At the same time, the good life has seduced upper- and middle-class people to invest in a senseless upward mobility that leads to empty lives—the promises of such a life are always false. Meanwhile, the lower economic class works at minimum wage or gives in to the welfare trap that so often makes fathers disposable and families dysfunctional. Maybe a real jungle would be easier to survive.

The Jungles Are Creeping into Our Schools

The jungles are destroying what is left of our villages. Schools, to use one commentator's words, are committing "fraud by promising a real education and delivering something much different."[5] The citizenry does strange things. One school district, while trying to merge two high schools to improve academics and finances, was opposed by the community because they didn't want to lose their football team, its colors, or familiar team names.

At a time when schools seem to be doing so poorly with more than 30 percent of entering college freshmen needing remedial courses, society is entering an era where higher levels of education will be needed for competing in a service-oriented, information-driven society. Meanwhile, the general public and corporate leaders are asking tough questions about school taxes: Should we pay more to get less? What a collision course.

Small wonder that so many have lost confidence in their schools. Sixty-two percent of respondents to a *U.S. News & World Report* poll think education kids receive across the nation is only fair, poor, or very poor. Asked the most seri-

ous problems, 34 percent say it is lack of parental involvement and 22 percent lack of discipline. In the same poll,
most people think the things that need fixing in schools
don't cost more money.[6] The schools can no longer be
counted on to provide basic skills, much less to shape enduring values.

How long can a society endure with declining education,
vanishing families, and disposable fathers? And does it not
follow that children of poorly educated, never-married parents will become unwed parents themselves, causing our
present family disasters to multiply in the coming generations?

Take Back What We Gave Up

All of this has to stop, but how? William Bennett puts the
problem in perspective:

> If we have full employment and a growing economy and jobs
> bursting out all over, but our children are dropping out of
> school, drinking alcohol, taking drugs, killing each other, get-
> ting each other pregnant, then it will not have been worth a
> candle. If we have cities of gold and alabaster but have not
> taught our children, or they have not learned, how to walk in
> goodness and justice and mercy, then we will have failed
> them, and the American experiment will have failed.[7]

If the church can't or won't do something, who will?

While things keep getting worse, our arguments about social policy get louder and political debates get shriller. We
talk a lot about welfare reform, gender equality, out-of-wed-
lock births, urban unemployment, minimum wage, and divorce. But something much more than talk is needed.

Something more than loud lament or continuous hand-wringing must take place. These issues, and a thousand more like them, have produced a frightening, entangling—even choking—soul-destroying force into our society. Just as weeds, varmints, decay, and dry rot take over abandoned buildings, wickedness and decay and avoidance overtake our families and churches. It's time to push back the jungle. To reclaim what we lost. To shout, "This is enough!" and make it stick. To refurbish our churches and communities with moral absolutes and everlasting truth and moral horse sense.

Even though the African proverb "It takes a village to raise a child" may sound poetic and idealistic, it does not go far enough. It is too diffuse and generic. It doesn't go far enough because everybody's responsibility becomes nobody's responsibility. That's where the church can make a difference.

Everybody's business is nobody's business. So government wants to leave children's issues to the school, the school to the home, the home to the community, and the community to the church. To change our children's future for the better, everybody has to exercise responsibility for children, and moral leaders must see the potential for good in the church. And to revolutionize our alarming situation, the church must report for duty.

As we have seen earlier, William Bennett clearly identifies the source of our difficulties. But are we really hearing? He says,

> Our problems are deeply moral and spiritual, philosophical and behavioral. They have to do with crime, murder, divorce, drug use, births to unwed mothers, welfare, child abuse, casual cruelty, casual sex, and just plain trashy behavior. And to

me, our largest crime in terms of the daily number of offenses is robbing children of their most precious gift: their innocence.[8]

Then Bennett offers the first step in taming the jungle:

We must be engaged with something more than economic policy. Economic policy matters. The founders of this country believed we were here in part to improve the material conditions of mankind. But they believed that the purpose of this nation was more than that. What is at stake today, I believe, is nothing less than our culture and our children— our civilization.[9]

Even Good Neighbors Are Not Enough

I (Neil) was raised in a close-knit neighborhood in Detroit where the community was really a metropolitan village. We were real neighbors and friendly helpers to one another. Illnesses, family crises, and deaths brought outpourings of help and authentic caring. The Buzenskis, Stubblefields, Kazakas, Greens, Blondells, Coffees, Berrys, Pickles, Binkleys, Alversons, and Nichols lived on our block. I could visit them anytime I wanted, and they sometimes offered me a cold drink or a snack. They paid me for mowing their grass in the summer or shoveling their walks in the winter. The postman and the policemen were our friends. We kids played kick the can in the street because there wasn't much traffic, and we played hide-and-seek at dusk. Before TV and air-conditioning, neighbors visited on their front porches, and we often stopped on our walks to or from church to admire a neighbor's flowers or to ask about the grown children or to give Mr. Berry a break from caring for his wife who, if she lived today, would be cared for in a nursing home or hospice.

But like any village, our neighborhood had significant limitations. A village, however broadly defined, can't do everything a child needs. After the snacks at neighbors' houses, I always went home to eat regular meals. Someone read to me at home. Someone taught me respect for others at home. Someone insisted I share family responsibilities there. Someone taught me to pray there. Some things the neighbors just can't do for a child.

As wonderful as our neighborhood was, it lacked something that home had. Home was more personal, more intense, more accountable, more lasting, and more loving than my neighborhood. I might have survived physically, emotionally, and spiritually without the neighborhood, but I could not have made it without family and home.

At home I belonged. Oh, how I belonged. By birth, by name, by relationship, I was part of the fabric of home. I was perpetual and not occasional. As good as they were, neighbors were never family or blood or relatives or kin. The family nourished me, knew me from my birth, took responsibility for me, and belonged to me. Those family strengths, missing in so many families and neighborhoods today, can be experienced in our churches if we intentionally build them into the churches' service to children.

Take a Second Look at the Church

Of course, Mrs. Clinton is right when she calls for everyone to search for something to take the place of families that are being blown sky-high by the millions every year, but a modern village—if you can find one—cannot do what needs to be done. However, the church can. Here's why.

Villages Are Vanishing, but the Church Is Still Here

Even though communities continue to look like villages, their relational characteristics seem to have disappeared while we were distracted. Neighbors no longer know neighbors. Most people can't name members of the city council or the school board, not to mention state legislators or nationally elected officials. Social distance, even among people who live in the same location, keeps growing.

However, unlike these evaporating villages, the church is still nearly everywhere present—about 350,000 congregations in the United States. And even though the church's influence may have waned, it can quickly be revived by intentionally reaching for five new children to love with the love of Christ, and then five more, and then five more. As one state legislator who upset an incumbent in a U. S. Senate seat race observed, "I was told over and over again, 'Don't run; this is David and Goliath.' I think they forgot David won."[10] Even when the church appears to be a David against the Goliaths of modern life, we can take back the ground and become the villages of God again.

Village Adults Don't See the Issues, but the Church Can

How can we say a village can raise a child when the majority of adults, especially parents who live in the proposed village, have never experienced a close relationship with neighbors, town, school, or God? Many experts in the social sciences claim much of our difficulties comes from parents who never had solid, well-adjusted families. Too many contemporary parents came from alienated, broken, or even dysfunctional families where home was a place to receive food and shelter but not a source of acceptance, encouragement, warmth, or moral development.

The church, in contrast, already functions in many places like an extended family where love and acceptance and togetherness are expressed and cherished. In many other settings, the church, with a little extra effort, can become an extended family resource for strengthening parents. It can become a place where substitute parents reach out to children who especially need them. It can become a place where caring adults find great personal fulfillment in loving children. In the church, stable family units help weaker family units by sharing the fact that their empowerment comes from Christ.

Villages Can't Always Be Trusted, but Churches Can

Consider all the trust children feel forced to give up in their upbringing in our time. They have to be taught not to trust a stranger, so when an adult tries to make friends with a four- or five-year-old on an airplane or in the aisle at Wal-Mart, the child looks with suspicion or even fear until his parent says, "It's okay to talk to the nice man." What a sad world when children have to distrust adults, but that's the way they have to be taught for their safety and for their parents' peace of mind.

Even though the church is sometimes held up to public and private ridicule over the moral decay of highly placed clergy, the church is generally trustworthy; and in most places a caring, morally cohesive Christian group leads local congregations. With few exceptions, the church can easily take the place of the former village, so when the village is extinct or can no longer be trusted, the family of God that meets at the corner of First and Main can become a child's moral and spiritual anchor. Children can trust, belong, and grow among their adopted family known as the family of God.

Villages Have Dying Institutions, Which the Church Can Replace

The problems we face in our institutions look and feel like southern Florida after Hurricane Andrew. Schools are on the ropes; some are intimidated by gun-carrying teens. The armed services are riddled with scandals. Social service agencies, intended to be dedicated to the care of the family and children, are charged with gross negligence. Health care costs are fleecing America.

The church, in such an environment, has opportunity to increase its credibility and show the power of righteousness. It is a good time for the church to show children and their families the spiritual reality they need—a time for the church to be the church and a time for the church to be reenergized for loving service to children and young people. The needed remodeling is not to start all over again, but to refuel and renew what John Powell in his book *The Secret of Staying in Love* describes so insightfully:

> My love must empower you to love yourself. We should judge our success in loving not by those that admire us for our accomplishments, but by the number of those that attribute their wholeness to our loving them, by the number of those that have seen their beauty in our eyes, heard their goodness acknowledged in the warmth of our voices.[11]

Everyone needs a church that loves like that—patterned after the love of fully: Christ. Those who need it will be magnetically drawn to the real thing.

Can the church tame this jungle? Of course it can. But it can't do it without concentrated effort, intentional commitment, and hard work—something like the all-out efforts our society makes in times of natural catastrophes or national disasters. That's what we face with our children—a heart-breaking national disaster.

NOTES

1. Bruce C. Hafen, "Marriage and the State's Legal Posture Toward the Family," *Vital Speeches of the Day,* October 15, 1995, 17.

2. Ibid.

3. Suzanne Fields, "A Youthful Breakdown in Morality," *Los Angeles Times,* November 1995.

4. Ibid.

5. Cal Thomas, *USA Today,* March 29, 1996.

6. *U.S. News & World Report,* April 1, 1996, 54.

7. As quoted in the *Gazette Telegraph* (Colorado Springs), October 6, 1993.

8. Ibid.

9. Ibid.

10. *U.S. News & World Report,* April 1, 1996, 23.

11. John Powell, *The Secret of Staying in Love* (Allen, Tex.: Thomas More Publishers, 1995), 102.

Chapter 3

IF I WERE A CHILD TODAY, I'D LIVE IN A HOSTILE WORLD

How Bad Is It?

How drastically childhood has changed from the time when Elizabeth Akers Allen wrote the poem "Rock Me to Sleep" more than eighty years ago:

> *Make me a child again, just for tonight! . . .*
> *Toil without recompense, tears all in vain,—*
> *Take them, and give me my childhood again.*[1]

Think of the positive changes for children in recent years. They do not suffer from diseases that used to kill many children. It is a fascinating world for them, especially for those who live in highly technological areas of the globe. They have knowledge of space exploration, laser beams, and the Internet.

But there is a darker side of the picture, too. Many people question any notions about idyllic childhood. Mountains of evidence suggest that childhood for boys and girls today is not the safe, secure, innocent time we have sometimes assumed it to be.

One fifteen-year-old put it this way: "All the kids I see

are in a rush to grow up, and I don't blame them. I don't think childhood is a golden age at all. I wouldn't want to be a child again."[2]

What has happened to cause "Make me a child again" to become "I wouldn't want to be a child again"? The answer is not difficult to discover. Try asking yourself, What might *my* life be like if I were a child now?

A Hostile World

If I were a child today, I would find the world increasingly hostile to me.

Through much of human history, children have been considered assets to a family. Verses such as Psalm 127:3, 5, which state, "Children are a heritage from the LORD, . . . Happy is the man who has his quiver full of them," reflected the general attitude of society toward children. Children have been valued for many reasons—as a means to carry on the family name, as contributors to the family livelihood, and as delights for their childlike ways.

Today, such a welcoming attitude toward children has changed. In technologically advanced societies, boys and girls have largely become consumers rather than contributors—and as a result, some people now regard them as liabilities. Not only are they expensive to raise—one estimate suggests that it costs nearly $200,000 to feed, clothe, and educate a child to young adulthood—but to many potential parents, children are serious obstacles to self-fulfillment, to being able to do "my own thing" and to being "my own person." Children are viewed as hindrances to a career and sometimes thought to be impediments to marital happiness. One childless career woman pointed out, "I have the time to see who I am, what I am, what I want, and where I want to go. I never could have done this with children. I would have felt trapped."[3] One grandfather who overheard her remarked acidly, "And she would have made her children terribly messed up emotionally and spiritually."

The growing antichild sentiment is reflected in many trends:

Language and definitions. A new language is springing up in regard to children. The term *child-free couple* is replacing *childless couple. Quantity time* is used to describe the time spent with children by the mother who does not work outside the home—implying mostly custodial care. *Quality time* is what the conscientious, hardworking, job-holding mother spends with her children after a day at work.[4] *Choice* is used in place of *abortion,* making the procedure appear to be a simple matter of preference. Some schools call students *clients* and talk about *accomplishment* rather than *learning.* And some sex researchers now refer to *child molestation* as *intergenerational intimacy.*[5]

Employment mobility. Large corporations, committed to earning the highest possible profits each year, pay almost no attention to the effects of multiple moves on the children of their employees. Every year, seven million children must change school systems in these moves. One youngster being treated for emotional problems had moved five times in one year. *U.S. News & World Report* recently published this report: "Typically, Americans change residences about a dozen times in a lifetime—twice as often as the French and British and four times as often as the Irish do. One reason for America's greater mobility is the divorce rate, among the highest in the world. The above-average mobility rates in Florida and the West reflect not only high divorce rates but continued strong migration into those areas."[6]

Housing. In the U.S., an increasing number of apartment

complexes ban children. Apartment managers cite noise and property destruction as reasons for these rules. A major percentage of the new housing being constructed is designed without considering children's needs. Sleek high-rise apartments represent a threat to a childlike way of life. Concrete parking lots are poor substitutes for grassy, tree-filled yards with places to experience the outdoors. And although a complex may house several hundred families, the design of the building prohibits warm neighborly relationships that used to flourish in traditional small towns and neighborhoods.

Why has the world become so hostile to children? Though several reasons might be cited, a major significant underlying cause is the determination of people to be free of the limitations on personal freedom that children—by their very nature—bring. Raising healthy children calls for large doses of self-discipline; self-sacrifice of time, energy, and resources; and self-giving love. All of these qualities create an incredible conflict with the philosophy of many in society, which says,

- Meet your own needs first.
- Find personal fulfillment.
- You have a right to happiness and a career.
- You have a right to everything you want.

Yes, if I were a child today, I would encounter a world that is becoming increasingly hostile toward me. I would want to grow up as quickly as possible, so I would not be such a bother. But that is not all.

A World of Broken Families

If I were a child today, I would more than likely see my family fall apart and have to learn to live with the terrible fallout. Elizabeth Kolbert summarizes our present situation:

> Divorce, longevity and deferred childbearing have all rendered what is now being called the "traditional family"— Mom, Dad and their biological progeny—increasingly exceptional. Fully a quarter of the children born in the 80's and 90's are being raised by single parents, and there are now more American households composed of people living alone and more households of childless couples than there are households consisting of married parents living with children. Since 1970, the proportion of "traditional" families has fallen by 35 percent.[7]

Meet Nancy. She is only eight and has already experienced enough broken relationships for a lifetime. She was conceived out of wedlock while both of her parents were still married to other spouses and they were parents of other children. Their marriage—when it finally did take place—lasted only a few years, just long enough for Nancy to become deeply attached to her father. Since the divorce, she sees him only on weekends. For a while after he divorced her mother, Nancy's father dated his former wife, Jill—but again, just long enough for Nancy to learn to love her. Now that relationship has broken off, and Nancy is learning to adjust to his new girlfriend, Sally. She also must learn to cope with her mother's new boyfriend and his children.

But it's not so much the people who keep entering

Nancy's life that give her emotional pain—it's those who leave. Although she cannot yet comprehend the reasons why, she has come to accept the fact that while Daddy is living with Sally, she can no longer visit Jill. It's easy to understand why Nancy wonders who will be the next to go. Her life is a cross between an emotional roller coaster and a relationship merry-go-round.

Divorce inflicts the worst imaginable kind of emotional abuse on children, but it continues as a result of our so-called enlightened ideas about multiple marriages. The thinking used to be that it was better for children to live in a divorced home than in a two-parent household with marital tension. Today, that view may be changing; some opinion shapers now suggest that no-fault divorce be abandoned so divorces will be harder to obtain. Both secular and Christian authorities agree that the effects of divorce are uniformly terrible for children.

Here are some of the problems divorce creates for children:

Undeserved guilt. Children of divorce suffer from powerful feelings of guilt. It often takes years to convince children that their behavior had nothing to do with their parents' separation.

Divided loyalty. Children of divorce suffer the tensions of divided loyalty. One youngster told David Elkind, author of *The Hurried Child,* "My dad tells me things about my mom and wants me to like him more than her. And my mom tells me things about my dad and she wants me to like her more than him. They get mad if I say anything good about the other one. I get tired of being asked which one I love the most."[8]

Some children in these situations learn to play one parent against the other. They appear to thrive on the chaos they engender by keeping their parents in a continual competition to win their favor; but underneath they are angry, afraid, and terribly insecure about life.

Loss of parents. Divorce actually means the loss of both parents for many children. Although children still live with someone they call Mom or Dad, it is soon apparent that the person is so preoccupied with the effort to cope after the divorce that there is little emotional energy left for parenting. Such parents often place additional stress on children by relating to them in ways that meet the parents' needs. As the fifteen-year-old said earlier, they feel forced to grow up quickly.

- These parents require children to function as partners who assume adult-sized responsibilities for housework, child care, personal supervision of activities, or completion of homework.
- They treat their children as confidants, telling them the details about their jobs or their dating, or expressing hostile feelings about the former spouse—the other parent of the children.
- They expect children to understand and accept behavior that is morally unacceptable by community standards, behavior that may include love affairs, children born out of wedlock, or welfare chiseling.[9]

Poor school performance. Children of divorce do much more poorly in school than do children from two-parent families.

One fact is abundantly clear: Children are deeply harmed by divorce. One sixth grade teacher observed,

You can walk into my classroom and easily pick out the kids from stable homes. Those are the kids who come in ready for school, ready to respond, ready to really work at things. The ones who are lacking this sort of support at home, especially those whose parents have just broken up and are busy with their own messy lives, are often very hyper. They seem to need an awful lot of attention. They want to talk to somebody, anybody, just to talk![10]

When God designed families, He planned that parents would provide their children with love and security, protection, moral and spiritual instruction, discipline, and emotional support in time of crisis. To reenergize the teaching of these values, the church must resource failing marriages by saying, "If your marriage is broken, fix it rather than junking it." It's time to help couples heal ailing relationships; rejuvenating a sick marriage usually takes much less effort than getting a divorce or remarrying.

Divorce, more than any other condition in society, leaves children defenseless in a world where boundaries are fuzzy, where relationships are distorted, and where security no longer exists. If I were a child today, I would worry about other boys and girls who have seen their families fall apart and are trying to cope with the results. And even though my home was stable, I might wonder whether divorce might sometime destroy my family.

A World of Guilty Parents

If I were a child today, I would live in a world where kids manipulate parents' guilt.

In a society where working parents have limited time for children, in a world where designer clothes and expensive athletic shoes top the list of artificial needs, and in a culture where cash registers at Toys R Us ring up sales nearly as fast as the food markets, some family specialists think kids set the priorities for family choices about churches, vacations, and cars.

Pastor Roger Thompson preached an intriguing sermon about this issue entitled "Kids Rule" in which he warned, "I wonder if we realize the massive shift that has taken place in the last forty years in this country. Do we understand how deeply we've been affected by the secular view of children? The bottom line is this: Kids rule and don't you question it."[11] He cautioned later in the same message, "Don't dare touch the educational philosophy of our land which says that children are on the throne. Parents line up; kids rule. Their wishes, their feelings, their happiness reigns supreme."[12]

Many people do not think children from affluent homes are at risk, but they are. The reason—their parents buy them everything and fail to help them believe anything. Harvard psychologist Robert Coles, a specialist in the effects of faith formation in children, brings these issues into crystal-clear focus:

> For fifteen to twenty years now, when I have asked American people what they believe in, they have said, "I believe in my children." Now when children have become a source of almost idolatrous, religious faith that is quite a burden for children to bear. Parents forget that what children really need perhaps more than anything else is discipline and a sense of commitment to something larger than themselves.[13]

Think of the spin-offs that come from affluent children controlling their families. Persons who plan and implement social policy often live as parents or grandparents with affluent kids who have strong influence or even rule their families. Such relational factors could have a bearing on shaping or misshaping policy for children in the culture, in the church, and in corporate America.

A World of Abuse

If I were a child today, I might be physically, emotionally, or sexually abused by those who are closest to me, namely, my parents or other close relatives.

A few years ago, *Newsweek* estimated that between 100,000 and 200,000 children would be molested that year.[14] That figure is undoubtedly higher now. One out of five girls is molested before she reaches adulthood, and 75 percent of the molesters are fathers or stepfathers.

Another two thousand to five thousand children die annually from physical abuse. In many cases, no one believes the child who reports abuse. Or if they believe, they treat the child as the offender. Three years ago, a tearful ten-year-old in a friend's fifth grade class confessed that her father was abusing her and her eight-year-old sister. When the teacher contacted the child's mother, she immediately took the child to a doctor where the abuse was confirmed. Following this, she placed the child in a foster home because she didn't want her.

Let's give child abuse a name and a face. *New York Times* columnist Bob Herbert helps us feel the pain:

The police report of March 5, 1990, refers to the arrival of a "DOA," a male black, approximately 5 years old, at Our Lady of Mercy Hospital in the Bronx. When cops first saw the boy, he was lying face up on a table in the emergency room. His body, which weighed only 35 pounds, was covered with thick welts, severe lacerations, and deep ugly bruises.

His head and lips were battered and swollen, as if he'd been in a prize-fight. The medical personnel tried to revive the boy but it was no use. He had been beaten so savagely his liver had split in two. He was officially pronounced dead about 9:45 A.M.

The police report recommended that the case "remain active," and it was:

The boy's name was Adam. He had been beaten by his father, Rufus, and his mother, Michelle, both of whom went to prison, and he was the subject of a celebrated "Frontline" documentary called "Who Killed Adam?"

. . . Adam had four siblings who ranged in age, at the time of his death, from eight months to 9 years. Except for the youngest child (the only girl), brutal beatings were routine and broken bones were commonplace. Child welfare officials had known since at least 1984 of the horror that was taking place in the household. . . . "Frontline" reported that Keith, who was two years old in 1984, had already suffered "a ruptured spleen, a perforated intestine, liver damage and fractures of the face, ribs, arms and skull." The mother was charged with abuse in mid-1984 and all of her children were taken from her, but only temporarily. She pleaded guilty to non-criminal charges of neglect, agreed to do better, and the children were returned.

It was like sending kids back into a blast furnace. Larry, a year older than Keith, would suffer a broken wrist, a broken leg and so many minor fractures the authorities lost count. Peter, the oldest child, reportedly tried to commit suicide after Adam's death, saying he wanted to join his brother in Heaven.

The city did not intervene in a meaningful way until Adam was killed. The surviving siblings were then placed in foster care. But except for the youngest child, for whom an adoption is being arranged, no permanent living arrangement has been worked out.[15]

What an abusive hell on earth some children experience every day of their lives.

A World of Violence

If I were a child today, I would live in a world of violence and fear.

Several years ago, a Hyde Park bank in the greater Chicago area sponsored a writing contest for children called "My Neighborhood" in which the bank expected to get a whimsical view of Chicago from the children's perspective. Much to everyone's surprise, the bank received stacks of essays and poems from frightened children. Listen to their fears, which the *Chicago Tribune* reported.

An eight-year-old boy titled his essay "Trapped in My House." He wrote, "I only go outside when I get in the car or go to school. I don't like my neighborhood because they shoot too much. They might shoot me so I stay inside."

A ten-year-old boy wrote a six-sentence essay including this sentence: "People get killed by shooting mostly every night."

Eleven-year-old Cynthia wrote, "We cry, we weep, we can't go outside and play because our parents believe we may be killed that day."

A fifth grade boy from the Raymond School wrote, "My neighborhood is like a jail. I am scared to go out because you are threatened that you will get beat up. And if you tell anybody you and the person you tell are going to get shot."

A thirteen-year-old wrote, "As you might know, I live in a slum. Some people call it hell on earth and so do I."[16]

Then there is also the problem of child-against-child violence. How can anyone forget the story of five-year-old Eric, who was dropped from the fourteenth floor of a public assistance apartment complex in Chicago by two other children, ages ten and eleven? The motive—the five-year-old refused to steal candy for the older children. In a terrible struggle, the young boy's eight-year-old brother, Derrick, tried to save him. The ten- and eleven-year-old boys had criminal records, and both said their fathers were in prison.[17]

Lest anyone think violence is limited to only one part of the country or one size community, here's a study reported from a national news magazine: "Currently, youths under 18 account for about 20 percent of the nation's violent crime. Demographic experts predict that juvenile crime will get considerably worse as a big new group of youngsters reach their teenage years."[18]

- There are more kids: "By the year 2010, the number of juveniles is expected to increase 31%."
- There are more drugs: "Although illegal-drug use among high school seniors had declined significantly since the 1980s, it began rising again in 1992."
- There are more guns: "Juvenile arrest rates for weapons-law violations increased 103% between 1985 and 1994."
- There are more murders: "The number of juvenile homicide offenders in 1994 was about 2,800, nearly triple the number in 1984."

The article concludes with this grim summation: "There is scant hope that the pessimistic trends will stop anytime soon. And tough speeches may be 'good for politicians' re-elections but don't make much sense,' says Jesse Williams, a Philadelphia youth-corrections official. The tragic fact is that it may take an even greater bloodbath to force effective crime solutions to the top of the nation's agenda."[19]

Of course, every child does not live in such violent surroundings, but too many do. Many children fear for their lives every day. And some of those fearful kids live in your town near your church.

A World of Television Addiction

If I were a child today, my closest friend might be my television set.

Fifty thousand schoolchildren were asked to tell which was more important to them—their television sets or their fathers. Over half chose the television set.[20] Is this an indication that today's boys and girls are heartless or spoiled? Not necessarily, but it does show the impact of TV on contemporary children.

Children obviously spend more time with TV than with their fathers. According to one study, fathers who were asked to tell how much time they spent with their children *reported* an average of fifteen or twenty minutes a day. When compared with six hours in front of a television, is it any wonder that children consider TV to be an important friend?

Why do children spend so much time in front of the TV set? One reason is that in many homes, the people children see and hear on TV are the only people present in the house for long periods of time. The Department of Labor reports that 32 million children under age eighteen have mothers who work outside the home. Another government report indicates that from 6.5 to 10 million children between ages five and thirteen are left alone at home after school or in the care of a preteen.[21] Of course, the length of time children spend by themselves varies, but one study showed that from two to three hours per day were typical. Children who are lost in a television program can temporarily forget that there is no one to talk to about their day, that they are scared, bored, or lonely.

So, what kind of friend do children have in television?

Television is a friend that inhibits the intellectual and social development of children.

Television is a friend that presents an unreal world. Consider, for example, Saturday morning cartoons. Children watch in amazement as one character after another is bashed over the head, run over, or blown up. That same character is back on his feet a few moments later racing to the next disaster. No wonder some children think that violence does no real harm, that it doesn't really hurt. Another tragedy in this unreal world of TV is seen more clearly when we remind ourselves that a personal Christian experience is based on the ability to trust. The ability to believe is one of God's precious gifts to children. But TV has potential to destroy or undermine the ability to trust.

What children don't see on TV is as much a cause for concern as what they see. According to a *USA Today* study, only 5 percent of those featured during prime time practiced religion, compared with 40 percent of the general population. Viewers saw no Boy or Girl Scouts and no one participating in service organizations such as Rotary or PTA. In several cases, a person portrayed doing "any of the hundreds of other activities that make up the bulk of the average . . . day" became the program's next "victim of violence."[22]

TV employs hard-sell techniques with youngsters who do not know the difference between a TV program and a commercial. By the age of six, children have seen about 120,000 commercials—most of them promoting salty and sugary foods or highly mechanized expensive toys.

TV saturates children with a non-Christian worldview. In the article "TV's Frisky Family Values," *U.S. News & World Report* published the following details. The article speaks for itself:

- Of 58 shows monitored during one week, almost half contained sexual acts or references to sex.
- A sexual act or reference occurred every four minutes on average during prime time.
- Actor Tom Selleck was quoted concerning a TV series on which he appeared, "I do have a dilemma: Can my daughter watch it?"
- A liberal producer was quoted as saying about TV comedies, "They seek to get away with as much as they can."
- Media Research Center found that portrayals of premarital sex outnumbered sex within marriage by eight to one.
- Even 58 percent of Hollywood's elite said TV should have more discussions of abstinence.
- Media Research Center notes that the network coverage of faith is almost nonexistent even when sitcoms have plunged into a state of family "dysfunctional overload."
- A study on four decades of entertainment TV reported about 50 crimes in every hour of prime time.[23]

These statistics cause alarm to all who have children's well-being at heart. Perhaps even worse is the fact that for many children, television has replaced parents as their primary value-shaper. How can this be? Here's how—the average child spends up to six hours a day in front of a TV set and only fifteen to twenty minutes with parents. It frightens one to say so, but if you were a child today, your closest friend would likely be a television set.

A World of Teen Pregnancies

A news magazine reports the following realities:

Since 1981, the federal Adolescent Family Life Program has tried to prevent teen pregnancies by encouraging abstinence. A study in last week's *Journal of the American Medical Association* suggests that the so-called Chastity Act project has fallen short. After five years of no growth in the early 1980s, teen pregnancy rates rose 9 percent from 1985 to 1990. . . . The obvious result: Birthrates soared. Six percent of all young women ages 15 to 19 had babies in 1990, a 13 percent increase since 1980.[24]

The article continues, "What's behind the higher rates? Some blame ineffective sex education, while others point to the fading stigma of adolescent sex and motherhood. But the costs and consequences are clear: Teen mothers are less likely to finish school and more likely to rely on welfare. Their pregnancies are more prone to complications. And their babies face a higher risk for prematurity, low birth weight, and death."[25]

What can the church do to change this cycle of brokenness? One veteran pastor said, "It seems our society is reaping astronomical consequences of breaking of the commandments for generations. At the same moment, the church, not wanting to seem judgmental, keeps still." He is right. How long can people of faith allow secular values to create such alarming problems for our civilization and our children?

A World of School Problems

If I were a child today, I would live in a world of troubled schools.

Corporations and citizens have begun raising difficult questions about our educational systems. Here's what the *London Times* reported about New York City schools:

> When President Bill Clinton condemned New York's school system as a bureaucratic "disgrace" last week, there was an angry response from the Big Apple. Clinton had been too kind, agreed everyone from Mayor Rudolph Giuliani down. . . . How bad have things become? Of the $5,300 spent annually on each student, a recent study concluded, most goes on teachers' salaries and administration and only $30 on books and classroom materials. But the city spends $160 per student on psychologists.[26]

Sounds like social and spiritual insanity.

Reporter Gregory A. Fossedal wrote in the *Wall Street Journal*, "Liberals would like the federal government to give more money to schools, while conservatives want less federal spending. There may be a way to make them both happy: cut down on regulations, mandates, and other costs imposed by Washington."[27]

American schools need to improve, and the improvement

is needed immediately. But while Johnny and Annie still can't read or write, decision makers are mired in states' rights, cutthroat funding competition, athletic priorities, and nonacademic social issues. In many places, meanwhile, high school graduates are not literate enough to complete job application forms, much less perform efficiently on a job or enter college. And in many schools, teachers say they can't get parents to return notes or attend parent-teacher conferences.

A World Where the Church Is Often Unfriendly

If I were a child today, I would live in a world where I did not always feel wanted at church.

Two thousand years ago, Jesus said, "Let the little children come to Me, and do not forbid them; for of such is the kingdom of God" (Mark 10:14). How well are we carrying out His wishes for children?

There are disturbing signs about how some churches view children. For example, a children's pastor was asked to take charge of a series of children's services at a neighboring church to be held simultaneously with adult services. When the pastor asked what kind of program the church preferred, the answer was, "We don't care what you do with them as long as you keep them out of the adult service."

A harried children's leader in another church says the most persistent problem is to find children's workers. Week after week, he places notices in the church newsletter begging people to help with Sunday school, children's church, and weekday Scouting. Week after week he receives a succession of "no" responses or resignations by people who say, "I don't want to miss regular worship services to serve children," or "I've worked with children long enough," or "I just don't have time to prepare," or "I did my duty when my children were young."

A national leader of children's ministries in one denomination tells about a letter she received from a woman who was heartbroken because the church decision group did not want the boys and girls she was bringing in on the bus to attend some church social functions. "They're too noisy and they don't know how to behave" was the reason given. So the teacher wrote for guidance on how to tell the children they were not welcome.

That same children's specialist remarked with frustration, "I see churches where the rooms for children are the shabbiest in the building. I see others where the rooms are beautifully painted and carpeted, but where teachers have been informed they are not to fasten anything to the walls for fear of marring the paint. I see churches where one frazzled worker struggles to teach a group of from twenty-five to thirty kindergartners—a class nearly three times the size recommended for effective teaching. I see churches where virtually no outreach to children is being made outside the existing adult membership. I see churches that find adequate funds for every concern except children. When I see such things, I realize that even in the church a child today might not feel welcome."

Could it be that some churches allow secular cultural views of children to color their attitudes toward children?

The secular view says, "Children cost a lot of money and do not bring us an immediate return on our investment." How often has the church said, "We want adults because they can pay their way"?

The secular view says, "Caring for children requires time, energy, and self-sacrifice. We don't want to make these sacrifices, so we don't want them." Some church people say, "Teaching children is too much work."

The secular view says, "Children are a block to my self-fulfillment." In the church, we sometimes say, "I can't work with children because I'll miss out on the other things in the church."

A psychologist once commented to Vance Packard, author of *Our Endangered Children,* "You can't do your own thing, search for your identity, and raise children at the same time."[28] Applying that idea to children and the church, we might conclude,

- you can't live a careless spiritual life and be a model of Christ for children.
- you can't think only of yourself and follow Christ's command to spiritually and emotionally care for children.
- you can't be guaranteed we will have a church tomorrow if you fail to minister to children today. If we want a family of faith in the next generation and we want people wonderfully centered on Christ, we must win the children.

Can You Hear the Children Crying?

What does all this mean? It simply underscores the graphic detail of a world that is no longer friendly to children and a world where children are no longer welcome. It describes a world where the children you see on the street or pass in a mall or notice on the playground can no longer count on love, security, and protection from people who should be providing these things for them. It describes a world where children who "survive" to teen years say, "I wouldn't want to be a child again."

The concerns of children must become nonpartisan if the nation is to survive. Columnist Suzanne Fields says reality outstrips our notions about politics when we realize "children really do like having a man around the house they can call Dad. . . . Little girls love to dance on Daddy's shoe tops and little boys like to toss the football around with him."[29]

Later in the same article, Fields sounds like a thundering prophet speaking to moderns:

> Experience eventually leads us all to reality. Those who indulged the free-wheeling morality of the '60s discovered that they didn't want their children to turn out like their parents. This comes with the insight of hindsight to parents who see clearly the sadness of children whose parents put their own "self-expression" and "self-fulfillment" first. Divorce, the growing numbers of single-parent families, the explosion of sexually transmitted diseases and the pandemic of teen-age pregnancies have robbed even the [political] left of its illusions. . . . Nuclear, as in family, is not so bad after all.[30]

The Church Minding Its Own Business

The church must lead in a new reformation to protect children even when critics holler their loudest, "Let the church mind its business." That's what we are doing—minding our business. Children are our business, even our main business. We all need to hear Jesus' clear-as-crystal warning again, "Take heed that you do not despise one of these little ones" (Matt. 18:10).

Children and their families, as never before, need genuine support and creative resourcing from communities, business, and government. But most of all, they need what only the church can provide. Every church that is redemptively responsive to the cries of the children can be a part of a revolutionary spiritual force for affecting the next generation and their parents with a satisfying life that flows from continual contact with Christ. The church must intentionally add a significant spiritual component to renewing a national nurturing of children, or the momentum of our present destructiveness will not even be slowed down.

God needs a reformer to champion the cause of children in your church and your community. Will you offer yourself for the challenge? Through the strengths of the family of God, we can resource, revitalize, and renew broken families. In the process, we can give thousands of children a new opportunity they will never have without us.

NOTES

1. Elizabeth Akers Allen, "Rock Me to Sleep," as quoted in *Bartlett's Familiar Quotations* (Boston: Little, Brown, 1980), 610.

2. Marie Winn, *Children Without Childhood* (New York: Pantheon, 1983), 207.

3. Vance Packard, *Our Endangered Children: Growing Up in a Changing World* (Boston: Little, Brown, 1983), 26.

4. Ibid., 23–24.

5. John Leo, "Who's for a Little Tongue Violence?" *U.S. News & World Report,* April 15, 1996, 23.

6. "Outlook," *U.S. News & World Report,* April 15, 1996, 18.

7. Elizabeth Kolbert, "Whose Family Values Are They, Anyway?" *New York Times,* August 6, 1995.

8. David Elkind, *The Hurried Child: Growing Up Too Fast, Too Soon* (Reading, Mass.: Addison Wesley, 1981), 44.

9. Ibid., 38–45.

10. Winn, *Children Without Childhood,* 141.

11. Roger Thompson, "Kids Rule," *Preaching Today,* May 1996.

12. Ibid.

13. Robert Coles, as quoted by Thompson, "Kids Rule."

14. Russell Watson et al., "Special Report, A Hidden Epidemic," *Newsweek,* March 14, 1984, 30.

15. Bob Herbert, *New York Times,* March 29, 1996. (Copyright © 1996 by The New York Times Co. Reprinted by permission.)

16. *Chicago Tribune,* December 14, 1992.

17. *Post Standard* (Syracuse, New York), October 15, 1994.

18. Ted Gest and Victoria Pope, "Crime Time Bomb," *U.S. News & World Report,* March 25, 1996, 28–36.

19. Ibid., 36.

20. From a UPI report in a Lincoln, Nebraska, newspaper; source unknown.

21. Packard, *Our Endangered Children,* 98.

22. "TV vs. Reality," *USA Today,* July 6, 1993.

23. Jim Impoco et al., "TV's Frisky Family Values," *U.S. News & World Report,* April 15, 1996, 58–62.

24. "Teen Pregnancies: High Rates, Higher Costs," *U.S. News & World Report,* April 15, 1996, 16.

25. Ibid.

26. *London Times,* March 31, 1996.

27. As quoted in *USA Today,* March 29, 1996.

28. Packard, *Our Endangered Children,* 28.

29. Suzanne Fields, "Even the Left Is Coming Around to Family Values," *Gazette Telegraph* (Colorado Springs), December 3, 1992.

30. Ibid.

Chapter 4

IF I WERE A CHILD TODAY, I'D NEED . . .

Developing Spiritual Kinship with Children

After we have discussed the alarming difficulties all children face, read books, and attended conferences, children still wait in our homes, in our churches, and in our communities for champions to improve their lives, to give them a future where they can know God, and to help them fully develop mind, body, and soul. They wait for people to speak for them and to represent them where they cannot represent themselves. They wait for people to show them Jesus—the children's Friend. They need a value-saturated environment in which to grow and learn. Children need us to make the Christian vision of how this world ought to be into a reality for them.

After admitting he knew many well-adjusted children, Vance Packard warned in his book *Our Endangered Children,* "The whole tilt of our society, our institutions and, yes, our family functioning is toward blighting our youngsters and burdening them with pain, anxiety, and discouraging problems. Many of these pains and problems threaten to create a permanent warping of a large segment of our coming generation."[1] Without even being faintly aware of these subtle trends, many people have changed their views about the value of children, about schools, about their personal priorities, and about the combined responsibility of all persons for caring for future generations. Many allow themselves to forget what every child needs the most.

To get the whole picture in sharp focus, think of one child you know. Get a name and face in your mind. Is his or her name Francisco or Tracey, Jose or Denise, Christopher or Maria? Personalize your focus so you are thinking about a specific child.

If you don't know a particular child, choose a child from today's newspaper whose distress appeared on the front pages. If you looked for a child like that in our local newspaper, you might choose a girl who missed by inches being killed in a drive-by shooting done by a fifteen-year-old gang member; a boy who burned down an apartment because he was playing with a lighter while his parents were at work; a boy who does not attend school because his parents are undocumented aliens; a girl whose father divorced her mother and insists on making the girl the subject of a bitter custody fight; or a child whose mother was called to military service in one of the world's political hot spots.

Abstractions don't help much when we are trying to understand what boys and girls feel by the long-term accumulation of our combined neglect of children. Many feel like victims of national policies that create as many difficulties as they solve. More policies and more social programs will not solve these difficulties. As future foundations crumble before our eyes, we must repair them quickly in every forum where we have influence. No longer can serious-minded Christians think that political systems will meet neglected children's needs. The time for all-out action has arrived. Columnist Rosemary Harris offers this call to holy arms:

> I see a crusade in this place [our city, Colorado Springs], an onward-soldiers kind of crusade aimed at saving our young people. Sometimes crusades make me suspicious. But I don't see anything fake, patently political, or self-serving about this one. There's too much at stake. We don't have to lose another child. Another one doesn't have to be hurt. Our city could be a model for what a galvanized community can do for its future. Its children.[2]

Let's make these issues precise, clear, and close by: If I were a child today, what would I need from the nearest Christian I know? What would I need from the church? What would I need from parents, extended family, society, and the community of faith?

I'd Need Adults Who Are Authentic Christians

Some churches major on public performance. Some churches emphasize praise without giving much attention to the content of the faith. Some churches follow traditional but empty forms. All three kinds of churches may have difficulty providing adult models of authentic Christianity for children. More than performance, praise, and tradition are needed to turn present theories about helping children into redemptive practices. Children need adults to show them Christ's love.

This modeling we envision must be done intentionally so that children know individual adults who have such an attractive Christ-quality life that children want to be like them when they grow up. During teen years when doubts develop, young people benefit by knowing persons who love them with Christ's love and have shown them by example how faith works in troubling times. William Bennett is right: "There is nothing more influential in a child's life than the moral power of quiet example. For children to take morality seriously they must see adults take morality seriously."[3] It's difficult for anyone, especially a child, to doubt the basics of Christianity when they are lived out before them.

In an address to the Helping Children Follow Jesus Conference at Wheaton Graduate School, Dr. Virginia Patterson, president of the Southern Baptist Pioneers Clubs, said,

In the past few years, studies have been done in the family systems discipline to determine why some children seem to be more resilient and survive when others in similar situations do not. In a Summer 1991 special edition of *Newsweek*, David Gelman reviewed this research in an article entitled "The Miracle of Resiliency in Children." The single most important factor for contributing to resiliency in children was a consistent, long-term relationship with a significant adult or adults.[4]

Children and teenagers never forget people who show faith and courage in their own living. Adults who lead in the church, adults who follow in the church, and adults who show an interest in children all have an important part to play in creating a future for a generation in crisis. Christian neighbors and family members have the opportunity to put an indelible imprint on the souls of children. At the same time, adults are enriched even as they serve children. Children and adults all benefit from the process.

I'd Need an Environment That Gives a Child High Priority

The ideal would be for the nation, schools, churches, communities, neighborhoods, and every home to cherish children and give priority to their development. Short of such an ideal, what can be done? People or groups in children's spheres of influence can cherish them. Every child needs at least one relationship with an adult that makes her feel special and important. Too often children, either accurately or inaccurately, feel unwanted at home, unwelcome at church, and hassled at school. Such children often live throughout childhood in loneliness. These are the children who most often join gangs, attach themselves to older sweethearts, or become lifelong loners.

By high priority, we do not mean more tinkering with social systems, although they are important. We mean the simple but significant priority of individuals who purposefully reach out to children. We mean adults becoming mentors to kids who have no adult influences. We mean intentionally including children without a family in your family's activities. We mean saying and doing things illustrated by this statement a single father made to several women in the church he attended: "I am a widower trying to be both father and mother to my children. I know I can't do it very well without help, but you have reached out to my daughters. Thanks for teaching them how to stand straight and walk like a lady and for including them in activities with your girls."

By high priority, we mean a childless couple becoming adult friends to someone else's child. In Neil's growing-up years, Iva and Charles Davidson were a childless couple who had married later in life, and for some reason they believed in Neil and his potential. About once each month, they took him home to Sunday dinner. They talked about what interested him. They talked about how to live and how to think and how to believe. They offered him a loan for his first semester in college. It is not hard to understand why they were among some of the most important people in his faith formation. They were friends of Neil's parents, but their friendship with the son was separate; it provided a richness of relationship that flowed both ways.

Mary B. lives out this principle in our city. Her children are grown, and she and her husband are in their retirement years. Our newspaper reported the other day that Mary feels a strong tie to the neighborhood school that gave her children a superior education. So, "most days you can find her at school, reading to children, helping them select library books, being a caring grand friend." The article continues, "It puzzles Mary that more retirees with time on their hands and public school success in their children's histories aren't doing the same thing."[5]

What has Mary learned that she could teach the church? She has learned the lesson that Margaret Mead, the famous anthropologist and authority on primitive cultures, taught, "Of course we need children! Adults need children in their lives to listen to and care for, to keep their imagination fresh and their hearts young and to make the future a reality for which they are willing to work."[6] Mary and Margaret have much to teach us all about the personal richness that comes to those who serve kids.

By priority, we mean helping a child learn to serve. Try taking a child with you when you visit a retirement home or when you teach a Sunday school class of nursery-age children or when you visit someone who is ill or when you go by to cut a disabled person's lawn. A family on my (Neil's) block sometimes shovel our walk early in the morning after a snowstorm but before we are up—think of what the children learn about neighborliness. But think also how much the children feel cherished when we brag on them and offer them money for doing such a good job. Some experts who write about the needs of children remind us that many boys and girls know nothing about serving. Why not take them with you when you do acts of service?

In a nearby town, a crew was assembled for an old-fashioned barn raising for a new church building. Can you imagine the impact it made on children who were allowed to do simple tasks, to eat with volunteers, and to help with cleanup? The building chairman for a new church in twenty years may be one of those children who collected wood scraps on that project.

As a child, I needed someone to cherish me as a person. I needed someone to put me in high priority and to let me see how important I really am in the whole scheme of society and especially in the church. So did you. And so do they.

I'd Need a Church That Allows Me to Be a Child

Contrary to what many people think, children are not small adults. Children think like children and act like children. Just as children always have, they copy our attitudes, our speech, and our actions. They must be taught to take responsibility for their actions, but we must all realize that today's children and teens are reaping a debauchery of yesterday's and today's adults' behavior. Much of the pathology of tomorrow will result from children being children who mimic what they have seen others do. Of course, we must also explore the positive side of that issue. Children who are raised with righteousness and fairness and generosity and love will likely become adults who reform society rather than destroy it.

In the church, we should expect children to be hard on buildings. It is foolish for anyone to believe that children's conduct will be perfect or that they will change to fit an adult world. Churches must intentionally plan pleasant space for children and recruit persons to serve children who understand that children will be children.

We have a wonderful dentist who practices family dentistry. His waiting room is designed to lower anxiety for his adult patients. He also provides a children's corner with an aquarium, a box of toys, and a whole shelf of children's books. Though going to a dentist isn't usually fun for children or adults, it is a joy to watch children come into that waiting room. The space and planning for children tell them we have been waiting for you, you are welcome here, we expect you to be a child, and we think you are special.

All churches, even the best ones, can be more child friendly than they are now. Look at your facilities. Check out the furniture and the bulletin boards. Evaluate the ministry to children. Does the whole environment say, "Children are welcome here"?

I'd Need Someone to Lower Antagonism Against Faith

Ignorance or outright antagonism concerning spiritual issues is real, and it affects a child in subtle ways. Let's be sure we do everything we can to counteract this reality. At Easter last year, three national news magazines ran pictures of Jesus on the covers but in the inside copy seemed more eager to report a new debate about the Resurrection by a small group of scholars against the two-thousand-year-old conviction of the creeds and Christians. The sidebars in those articles talked about reinventing Christianity when our greater problem is that Christianity has all but been removed from our society while millions continue to believe and live by its beliefs.

Let's realize that a kind of public disbelief scoffs at faith and questions anyone who believes anything positive about Christ and the Bible. In his book *The Devaluing of America,* William Bennett tells about a time when Mike Wallace sent a crew from CBS to follow him for weeks soon after he had become secretary of education. The idea was to give Bennett enough rope to hang himself regarding his religious commitments. After shadowing Bennett for three weeks, Mike Wallace asked Bennett into his office for a casual conversation. At the end of the interview, Wallace asked the knockout-punch question, "Do you believe an American child should be able to leave an American public school without the belief that Jesus Christ was his personal Lord and Savior?" Bennett answered, "Absolutely. That's not the purpose of a public school. Unfortunately, he can leave many of our public schools and not know lots of things that school is supposed to teach him." Wallace was so upset that he picked up his stack of papers and remarked to his producer, "We don't have anything." The story never ran on *60 Minutes.*[7]

Children need to be taught faith and wholeness. They need to be taught that breaking the commandments always produces harmful consequences. They need to have the harsh edges of criticism of faith blunted and the unsatisfying results of secularism highlighted through what they see in people of faith and what they are taught at church and at home. Faith in the Lord Jesus Christ makes people strong and loving and caring even though the media sometimes try to make them appear weird or off center. Of course, there are exceptions—but that is true of every occupation and reality in the universe.

Let's unashamedly teach children that life always goes better with Christ. Even for persons who apparently have few needs, their lives will have more meaning and significance when they are centered on Christ. For those whose lives seem filled with despair and crises, they are better for having lived near Christ, their Strengthener and Enabler.

The antagonism to faith in contemporary culture is real. To counteract it, we must feed children faith if they are to have a tomorrow of meaning. Our land cannot continue to be the land of the free and the home of the brave and a place of spiritual vitality without Christian people doing everything we can to help children see through the antagonism against faith that pervades much of our culture.

I'd Need Someone to Strengthen or Supplement My Family

In the notion that it takes a village to raise a family, the ideal of the extended family is absolutely necessary, but the extended family doesn't always work very well these days because so many people live many miles from grandparents, uncles, aunts, and cousins. Add to this loss of the extended family the number of broken biological families, and we have big problems. The breakdown of the American family over the last three decades has been disastrous for children and has increased social problems that rob children of security and emotional support at the time both are most needed.

Come Alongside to Strengthen Marriages

Barbara Dafoe Whitehead summarizes the problems caused by our weakened family structures:

> Children in single-parent families are six times as likely to be poor . . . are two to three times as likely to have emotional and behavior problems . . . are more likely to drop out of high school, to get pregnant as teen-agers, to abuse drugs, and to be in trouble with the law. . . . Many children from disrupted families have a hard time achieving intimacy in a relationship, forming a stable marriage, or even holding a steady job.[8]

Another columnist says it so well, "In light of the data, people can . . . no longer honestly maintain that divorce and single-motherhood are good for kids. . . . There is a reality that must be faced: For most children, growing up with only one parent is economically, psychologically, and emotionally harmful."[9] We also must add that growing up without biblical training, a sense of belonging in a church, and a guiding center—Christ—for living is destructive and leads to an empty life.

Look at these statistics:

- Seventy percent of all juveniles in state reform institutions come from fatherless homes.
- The presence in classrooms of children with emotional crises at home undermines the mission of schools.
- Preschool children in stepfamilies were forty times more likely to suffer abuse than children in intact families.[10]

What a list—one that can be expanded from hundreds of other surveys.

One thing is sure. Divorce hurts kids. Almost every party to the discussion of the problem will acknowledge the position Sheila Lawlor took in a *London Times* article about family breakdown worldwide: "Divorce on its present scale has a bad effect on those involved and deleterious long-term effects on the children." Then she asks the question of all questions, "Must we simply accept these socially damaging consequences of a high divorce rate as the unfortunate result of modern ways of life?"[11] The church must answer with a resounding no in its teaching and preaching and impact on society in general. The 1995 report, "Marriage in America: A Report to the Nation," advises, "The time has come to shift the focus of national attention from divorce to marriage and to rebuild a family culture based on enduring marital relationships."[12] We think it's past time, and the church is the only institution in the present scheme of things that can pull it off.

Love Children from Broken Families

In addition to strengthening marriages, the church must serve children who have been victimized by divorce. The church can become the family of God to these children and to their parents. One mature churchwoman said, "We know how to love hurting, rebellious teenagers because we have had so much experience with our own and with those of our church family." Every child needs a church to love her. Every child needs a church to help her intact family do better parenting, and thus to give her a happier, more stable home, or to come alongside her broken family to become the family of God for her.

President Jimmy Carter's advice speaks seriously to the

church and to its care for the young in our society: "During my lifetime, a profound change has taken place within the organic family structure that deprives many children of the nurture and stability they need. Although our general society therefore has a greater role to play, there is a disturbing lack of either attention or wisdom focused on this most crucial challenge."[13] That's what this book seeks to do—focus attention on this most crucial challenge.

Become a Substitute Family

David A. Hamburg, M.D., opens his book with this powerful sentence: "Today's children are in crisis because today's families are in crisis."[14] That's the church's issue. Children suffer, and we must do something about it. The issue is not what should be done, but what is being done. And the church is called to respond to this crisis in every possible way so that every child is connected to the family of God either through his own family or through others becoming like a family to him. To use Wendy's restaurant president Dave Thomas's words, "Thousands of children dream of being in a family portrait." The church can make that portrait possible for such children.

Saving a child at any cost is our task. If that means picking up the pieces, we should do it. If that means teaching parents how to be parents, we should do it. This should be done in a loving congregational setting where the church is such a joy-filled place that one would be pleased for the church family to be her real family.

Help Parents Who Fail at Parenting

Losers at parenting need the church's attention, too. James Webb—novelist, former secretary of the navy, and father of four—wrote in *Newsweek* just after his daughter left for college:

> My daughter grew up listening to the disagreements of her parents, both before and after their divorce. She learned what it meant to be a "latchkey kid," cared for by phone. She heard those who celebrated the drug culture tell her "just say no" about the time that high-school drug dealers started wearing beepers to class. She knows that the generation that flaunted sexual freedom is queasy now, what with abortion so common among teenagers and their illegitimacy rate triple that of 20 years ago.[15]

Webb then wrote words that sound like a statement of old-time repentance:

> Mine has not been a generation that offered its children certainties. We have treated them to endless argument instead. . . . My daughter has been treated to a view that government is corrupt and unfair; this was fed by continuous debates over civil rights, the Vietnam War, Watergate, and the Iran-contra affair. She has also watched the nation blunder about in its role as world leader, jerked this way and that on foreign-policy issues and by leaders who appear to be selling her future to foreign investors instead of calling on its citizens to regain the self-discipline that made us great. . . . We the members of a creative, sometimes absurd, always narcissistic postwar generation, will soon receive a judgment. Whatever it is, our children have earned the right to make it.[16]

People who have long second thoughts about their parenting efforts need a church to demonstrate to them the benefits and wholeness found only in the living Christ.

I'd Need a Loving Sunday School Teacher

Mary Quackenbush made a serious faith commitment to Christ when she was seventy-five years old. She became an enthusiastic, dedicated, faithful teacher of ten-year-old girls.

Surely, if anyone had valid reasons for not teaching children, Mary had them. But Mary taught week after week. And then there was the matter of experience. There were probably occasions when Mary as a young Christian could not answer the kinds of questions that junior girls can raise. But there she was, studying her lesson faithfully, consulting with her pastor when necessary, and trusting God for the wisdom to deal with those questions wisely.

How did Mary approach her task of teaching the junior girls? Was she there only because the church was short of workers? Only because she felt a sense of guilt or duty? No, she was there because she loved children and wanted to make a difference in their lives. I know. I (Neil) pastored Mary and caught her enthusiasm for ministry as I spoke with her.

Being a Sunday school teacher is a lot like Fred Barnes's idea about being a father:

Fatherhood isn't brain surgery. I say this in defiance of the new conventional wisdom that being a father is breathtakingly difficult, that it creates tough dilemmas and that fathers need a strategy for carrying out their duties. I don't think so. Most men I know have an instinct for fatherhood that was triggered the day their first child was born. They instantly recognized the No. 1 requirement of fatherhood: to be there.[17]

The number one requirement for a Sunday school teacher is to love children, and that spiritual instinct is learned from close association with our loving Lord.

I'd Need Someone to Speak Up for Reforms

Just now, Christians all over the country are making their voices heard and their votes count in national and local elections. Many who oppose this new force for righteousness have influenced elections for years but are now calling these new efforts a foul ball—as if making public officials aware of the citizens' concerns was not as old as America and a healthy expression of democracy. After all, the cornerstone of our national life is government by the people and for the people.

More individuals and more groups must represent children in halls of government and in halls of schools. Many other special interest groups have representatives and funding sources to make their wishes known to elected officials, but children must count on adults to speak for them. Though they are children for such a short time, what happens in childhood shapes them forever. The nation must have better schools, of course; but the church must speak up, not to control the votes, but to be sure truth and right and values are built into the fabric of America. Of course, Christian people will not agree on every detail of every issue, but they can produce a groundswell to ensure that righteousness serves as the controlling factor for all public policy.

Gerry Spence, the nationally known attorney, is waging a war against the tobacco interests in the nation. He calls them peddlers of dope that enslave millions of young people who start to smoke in early teens as a result of peer pressure and subtle advertising. He has named national civic leaders who were lobbied by the tobacco industry and accepted campaign money. Addiction, early death, suffering, financial stress on the nation's medical resources, tobacco subsidies, and many other issues growing out of this debate should be centered on what is right and what is just and what is true.[18] Efforts like that affecting children need the attention of the church and of its many members.

Parade magazine ran an article about the 1996 Stand for Children Day at the Lincoln Memorial. The article called "Let's Make It Happen" by Michael Ryan opens with a story about a church in Lynn, Massachusetts, where a child was killed near a church—a terrible tragedy. The minister and church members went down to city hall and said, "We need some place for our children to go. We need to give them things to do." When the city council told them there was no money, they asked for a copy of the city's budget. They thought that anyone who could read a church's budget might be able to read a city's budget. When they did, they found expenditures that could be cut to free up money to fund recreational activities. Under positive pressure, the budget priorities were changed.[19] When those church members in Lynn did that, they were doing what every church everywhere has to do—stand up for children in every forum where it counts. The organizer of Stand for Children Day, Marian Wright Edelman, is right: "It isn't enough not to hurt children. We have to begin thinking about helping them."[20]

The needed reforms call for action as well as talk. *New York Times* reporter Kirk Johnson filed an essay about a wonderful example of reforming action involving veteran public school teacher Gary L. Fitzherbert of the Devereux

Glenholme School near Danbury, Connecticut. Fitzherbert offers character training in his classroom based on six bedrock principles of good conduct: (1) trustworthiness, (2) respect, (3) responsibility, (4) fairness, (5) caring, and (6) citizenship. Connecticut was the first state in the Northeast to declare a Character Counts Week. Though we do not know enough about this particular program to recommend it, the idea of character education in public schools seems like a very good one. However, we wonder how it can be done without a faith component.

Whatever shape such a program might take, there is some evidence that a wider number of local community leaders realize something must be done about character development—right and wrong do exist independently of how we squabble about it. Mr. Fitzherbert sounds like a churchman when he says we have abdicated our obligation to educate children about right and wrong.[21] Maybe it was television, or maybe it was the anxiety to avoid conflicts of church and state, but we walked away, and we must now return. Speaking up for righteousness and morality as a basis for reform is something the church must do more effectively and more frequently.

A commitment to insist that the needs of children be considered in all public forums has to be on the church's agenda because of its commitment to children. Physician Lee Salk once wrote with passion, "The cost to society of children whose lives have been damaged by poor nutrition, poor educational opportunities, poverty and poor health management is devastating. Ignoring these problems in the face of all the knowledge we have about the factors that contribute to their causes is beyond belief when we think of the resource, power and supposed wisdom of our elected officials."[22] Every word of Dr. Salk's statement is true. But his outrage must be broadened to include spiritual commitments and moral issues. Like leaders in the early church, "we cannot but speak the things which we have seen and heard" (Acts 4:20).

NOTES

1. Vance Packard, *Our Endangered Children: Growing Up in a Changing World* (Boston: Little, Brown, 1983), 26.

2. *Gazette Telegraph* (Colorado Springs), April 13, 1996.

3. William J. Bennett, *The Book of Virtues,* as quoted in *Reader's Digest,* February 1996, 47.

4. Unpublished speech delivered at Wheaton, Illinois, date unknown.

5. *Gazette Telegraph,* April 8, 1996.

6. Hillary Rodham Clinton, *It Takes a Village* (New York: Simon & Schuster, 1996), 6.

7. As reported by Ravi Zacharias, "If the Foundations Be Destroyed," *Preaching Today,* no. 142, 1.

8. As quoted by Mona Charon, *Gazette Telegraph,* March 29, 1993.

9. Ibid.

10. Ibid.

11. Sheila Lawlor, "Managing Modern Marriages," *London Times,* April 6, 1996.

12. As quoted in *Current Thoughts & Trends,* March 1996, 13.

13. David A. Hamburg, *Today's Children* (New York: Times Books, 1992), back cover.

14. Ibid., 19.

15. James Webb, *Newsweek,* November 7, 1988, 13.

16. Ibid.

17. As quoted in "Points to Ponder," *Reader's Digest,* September 1995, 191.

18. CNBC broadcast, April 7, 1996.

19. Michael Ryan, "Let's Make It Happen," *Parade,* April 7, 1996, 5.

20. Ibid.

21. Kirk Johnson, "Character Is Making a Comeback," *New York Times,* August 6, 1995.

22. Lee Salk, *Familyhood* (New York: Simon & Schuster, 1992), 191.

Chapter 5

REDISCOVERING THE VILLAGES OF GOD

Making Your Church Child Sensitive

First Lady Hillary Rodham Clinton speaks passionately in her book *It Takes a Village* of the pressing need for contemporary society to rediscover and use the relational qualities of a village as a miracle force for nurturing the next generation of adults—our children. As we have seen, children are at incredible risk in our society. The evidence surrounds us like the blackest midnight.

Mrs. Clinton is right to remind the nation how much children need more hope and more help and a greater sense of home. Boys and girls need to receive such a sense of belonging from those who know them best, those who live closest to them, and from society in general. These somber thoughts from her pen should be considered a call to arms—to do as much as we can right away: "They [the issues about children] are intimately connected to the very essence of who we are and who we will become. Whether or not you are a parent, what happens to America's children affects your present and your future."[1]

The Moral Swamps Are Drowning Us

These needs are gigantic. Illegitimate births have risen 400 percent since 1960, and the males who father these children are almost never meaningfully involved in raising them. Divorce rose 352 percent from 1960 to 1990, so only 62 percent of our children in the United States now live with both biological parents.[2] The problem becomes ever greater when emotional absence and spiritual neglect and frequent adult absences are considered. All these realities drive up instances of teen suicide, mental illness, violence, drug use, and sexually transmitted disease because youths with these difficulties, as a group, are sexually active earlier and have more partners.

Children Need a Village of Grace

Our children need a community of like-minded adults to value them as worthwhile persons for the present, as well as to cherish their potential for the future. Our children need a society to protect them from the mental and emotional garbage that comes through TV and other media sources. Our children need acceptance and affirmation. Our children long for security and a return of innocence. Our children need authentic, wholesome, well-adjusted adults to help them become all God intends them to be. Our children are desperate for a whole network of persons—an extended family—to show them love that nurtures and nourishes the whole being.

When we first heard the title of Mrs. Clinton's book, we felt an exciting agreement that someone was speaking up for children, their rights, and their future. I (Neil) even remarked to a friend as we browsed at Barnes and Noble Bookstore, "What a wonderful concept—an idea whose time has come. A caring community is exactly what millions of children need right now." Then I thought again, *Children won't wait. Each new growth stage comes, ready or not. Tiny infants rapidly grow into boisterous children and then into choice-making teens and then . . .* That's when I began to realize how few villages we actually have left.

Kay C. James, dean of Robertson School of Government at Regent University, Virginia Beach, Virginia, explains why the villages have almost disappeared:

> Where once neighbors and friends comprised a community, now we are afraid to walk down our own street. Where once the only way to meet the enormous challenges of being black in America meant reliance upon fellow African Americans, today the rise of black-on-black violence has reached epidemic proportions. Previously, families facing hard times could rely upon relatives and friends to help make it; today the sight of homeless men, women, and even children is all too common.

> What does this say about our *village*? It says it is gone; that it has been utterly and completely destroyed. Worse, all of the effort and money that has been thrown at our social problems has done little to halt its destruction.[3]

Where Did the Villages Go?

Then I thought about our global village with its incredible communication links so we have almost instant news when a madman kills young children, flags are being burned, a plane crashes, or another terrorist strikes fear into the heart of the world. Now we get faster news about people in other parts of the world than people used to get about their next-door neighbors. But since we have so few ways to help in these desperate situations—no way to bind up the dying wounded or to significantly change the world—we get calloused to reports that seem so depersonalized and so far away. We don't mean to, but we do. That same process often happens when we get information about the needs of children in our time.

As we thought more about this village idea, we started wondering where one could find a village in which people genuinely cared about children. By dictionary definition, a village is a small settlement of homes and families, considerably smaller than a town. Sometimes the word *village* is used to describe the inhabitants of such a community.

Near the same time I (Neil) was processing this whole village issue in my mind, I drove across western Kansas where the small towns are shrinking. I even stopped at a Dairy Queen near one of those tiny towns to get the feel of the place and talk to people. They said the farms are getting bigger and the population is getting smaller. It seems that most villages are either gone or quickly disappearing.

But something even more basic than the village is the associations and connections of persons in families. Even Former President Lyndon B. Johnson, thought by many to be the granddaddy of many failed social experimentations for children, realized the basic solutions start with families:

> The family is the cornerstone of our society. More than any other force, it shapes the attitudes, the hopes, the ambitions, and the values of the child. And when the family collapses, it is the children that are usually damaged. So, unless we work to strengthen the family, to create conditions under which most parents will stay together, all the rest—schools, play-

grounds, public assistance, and private concern—will never be enough.[4]

Churches have lost the village touch, too. Some seem involved in becoming big institutions or growing bigger crowds; others are dying out as the older generation passes with no one to take up their spiritual and economic mantle; still others are in a survival mode, trying to keep the bills paid and the doors open but not involved much at the cutting edge of congregants' lives.

Not only have children been let down and abused by all of this, but leaving them out has damaged the spiritual and mental health of the country and the church as well. The real situation we face with vanishing villages is explained by Kay James:

> Unfortunately, rather than work to rebuild the *village,* we have instead taken the broken bricks of families, the mortar of cultural institutions, and the steel of houses of worship and used them to build up Town Hall. Too many of our "leaders" confidently make the claim that where our community has failed, government can and should step in. . . . Not only is Town Hall a poor replacement, it has played a major role in destroying the *village*. Dependency upon what government offers—whether empty rights or degrading welfare— has robbed us of the drive so necessary to sustain and strengthen the institutions of the *village.*[5]

Government can never do what the family and the church were planned to do.

Then Gary Bauer's perspective about big government not being anything like a village must also be factored into our thinking:

Big government isn't a village. And bureaucrats in Washington are not better able to make decisions for children than loving parents. The village must be an environment in which families are supported and strengthened. The problem today *is* the village. Cultural pollution, crime, violence, liberal government policies, sexually explicit images, unresponsive educators, and anti-faith bigotry are among the "village forces" that work against families trying to teach their children right from wrong and trying to give them a sense of the American dream.[6]

If it takes a village to raise a child, how can villages be recovered or created? Let's get specific. How can families on welfare in East Los Angeles locate a village to nurture their children? How can a single mother in Manhattan find a village or create one? What do folks do to find a sense of community when their situation is like that of the young doctor who took early retirement from the military to relocate in a new housing suburb where people see their neighbors only as they drive off to work in the morning or as they punch their garage door openers from their cars at the end of the day?

The list goes on and on. How do we find a village for a crack-addicted newborn baby who is a victim of the sins of her mother? Let's think about how to locate a village for Sam's children; his wife deserted the family, leaving him with two preschool-age children while he tries to finish college. How do we find a village for the thirteen-year-old prostitute in downtown Indianapolis propositioning a man in his late thirties while sucking her thumb?

Problems the Village Idea Creates for Us

Too often, "it takes a village" merely turns out to be a subtle call or even a code word based on a faulty assumption that the family and the family of God can be replaced by government or governmental agencies. They can't because

- no village can impact a child that does not encourage stable families as the norm.
- no village can impact a child where congregations teach there is no absolute truth or eternal issues.
- no village can impact a child that allows its people to think what they believe does not affect how they behave.
- no village can impact a child where schools are judged by a student's socialization rather than by actual learning.
- no village can impact a child where the most important institutions of society are replaced by government.
- no village can impact a child where regulations are more important than relationships.

We love William Raspberry's story of a couple who go to a restaurant to recapture an enchanting evening from their past. Years have passed and many discouraging events have taken place, but they think the restaurant can bring back the old feeling. So they go to the restaurant and no feeling comes.[7] Sooner or later, it might be well for the couple to realize the enchantment of the past was the relationship, not the restaurant. Maybe we need to seek the relationships a village provides rather than the village itself. It's not a village we need so much as what the village did for us in relationships—a sense of loving and a place of safety. The things we yearn for cannot be provided by politicians or governments. God and friends and relationships with people of like mind such as we find in the family of God provide them.

Why Not Use Our Villages of God?

By villages of God, we mean all the churches and social agencies and homes that have joyously embraced Christ as their guiding center. The idea is bigger and smaller than a coming together of churches. But why not start with churches?

If this proposal sounds too utopian or socially naive, the idea is supported by an article entitled "Kids Who Scare Cops." The article presents these alarming statistics: "Between 1985 and 1992, the rate at which males ages 14 to 17 committed murder increased by about 50% and over 300% for blacks. Currently, there are about 40 million children under the age of 10, the biggest number we have seen in a decade. By the year 2005, the number of males in the 14- to 17-year-old age group will have risen by 25% overall and 50% for blacks."[8]

The article also quotes a veteran police officer as saying, "I never used to be scared. Now every time I get a call at night involving juveniles, I pray I go home in one piece to my own kids."[9]

The same article also offers support for using the villages of God to save our children:

Experts agree that the greatest factor is that many of these children are growing up in moral poverty. No one is teaching them right from wrong. No one is teaching them compassion for others. No one is teaching them to even think about others, let alone care for others. In fact, all they have seen modeled for them is an adult world full of violence and chaos and abuse. . . .

What can be done to avert this tragedy? Mounting evidence is pointing to religion as an effective antidote to these problems. A 1986 study by Harvard Economist Richard Freeman showed that among urban black youth, church attendance was a better predictor of who would escape drugs and crime than any other factor. We need to provide public funds to support local religious institutions that provide a safe haven for at-risk children. Our guiding principle should be: build more churches, not more jails.[10]

Consider the incredible possibilities. While the public funding might be debated, with almost no cost, but with lots of imagination and creativity, the churches of our land could put the national problem of children in a much higher place on their agendas. They probably would if they truly realized the crisis we face and that they really can make a difference.

Churches everywhere—both large and small—could improve the problem quickly by finding ways to touch the next generation. It would be a Save the Children campaign where every child is seen as a valued member of the family of God. Children in the congregation would be loved for who they are. Children in the community would be touched and cared for and won to Christ because it is right and it needs to be done. And parents would be grateful, too—people who care for children are always loved by their parents.

Megachurches might lead the way by establishing one-on-one relationships between children and church members; the goal would be for every adult to have a friendship with a child—something like the godparent idea when it worked at its best.

No church is too small to assign every member a personal caring ministry to a child. Children from church families, both outside and inside, would be given an adult friend at church who would pray for them, nourish them, and inquire often about the state of their faith.

Everyone can be involved because everyone has experience. After all, everyone knows how a child thinks because they were one once. The idea is to renew the church to be like what former chaplain of the U.S. Senate Richard Halverson described, "In the beginning, the church was a fellowship of men and women centered on the living Christ. Then the church moved to Greece, where it became a philosophy. Then it moved to Rome, where it became an institution. Next, it moved to Europe, where it became a culture. And finally, it moved to America, where it became an enterprise."[11] We, too, want the church to go back to the family fellowship stage when the early church seemed like a village of friends who genuinely cared about one another and their children and who were committed to a world-changing task. It can be done. The church did it once when it had only a handful of members in a hostile social environment. What could the church do with millions in our time?

A megachurch anywhere could take on the responsibility to reach out to as many children as it has adult members. That could result in thousands of children being touched with the love of Christ by one congregation. A tiny village of grace can be started by larger churches on every street where any of their people live.

A new church plant might reason that members have to serve children if they are going to justify their existence in the new setting. The church is on its way to being firmly planted when the community starts saying, "The new pastor and the new church love our kids, so it is not hard to love them back. This is the kind of warm family feeling that I want my children to experience."

Some churches could challenge their golden agers to establish contacts with children—perhaps by mail and phone. Soon children will visit their substitute grandparents, and as a result the child, the church, and the golden agers all are helped.

Where Can the Villages of God Be Found?

Villages of God are not hard to find because they are everywhere. Two or three Christian people in a neighborhood could start an effort near their home. A village of God to care for children might provide a service focus of prayer for a women's or men's prayer group. A village of God might start with an adult Sunday school class showing interest in caring for children.

A young pastor in our town went to visit a young teenager in the hospital who had been injured at school by a drive-by shooting. Though he did not know the girl or her family, he thought they might not have a church, and he was right. When he introduced himself at the hospital, he said, "I care about you and all the teens of our community. I've come to cry with you and to pray if you want me to do so." He made a hospital room a village of grace the teen and her parents will never forget.

One church uses prayer groups as a way of getting focus for new ministries. The prayer groups study Scripture and pray together once each week. As they pray for a special need, God often gives them guidance about what they must do to answer their own prayers. Such prayer-study-service groups could be urged to pray seriously and specifically about the problems of children in their community. One member of the group might be asked to gather prayer requests for a week from newspaper articles that show how children are being mistreated in their town or city. Strategies for serving children will grow out of their seeking divine guidance.

The concept of villages of God is not to create programs, but to put a new emphasis on building healthy, Christ-centered relationships with some of the most needy persons in the population—our children. The idea is to refocus the direction of a church away from institutional preservation and on to authentic human needs. It means offering to come alongside parents.

The good news: Being a village of God to children is something the church already knows a lot about, and the facilities are already in place. Many adults in every church were loved to Christ by someone when they were children. So many know how to replicate what happened to them as a ministry to the new generation.

Challenging your church to be a village of God is actually challenging the church to be what God meant for it to be. Play down this idea as another program, and emphasize the efforts to revolutionize the next generation. This is a big-brother and big-sister relationship to grow spiritually strong people for the next generation. Remember, all spiritually homeless children do not live on the street—some of them live in high-priced homes in the best neighborhoods.

Challenge Individuals to Try

With apology to editor Mike Bullock of the *Chaffee County (Colorado) Times,* I have paraphrased a part of one of his editorials. Challenge everyone in your village of God to start thinking about children this way:

> I have a feeling I am important to the next generation, and that awareness challenges me to do everything I can to impact a child. To touch a child with Christian impact is to help shape the future. I plan to encourage every child I meet. Then when that child sees God's love in me, he or she will show it to others—perhaps now as well as in adulthood. He or she will touch others whom I will not see.

> By caring for one child, I may impact hundreds of people in the next generation who will touch many others with the holistic power of Christ. I will be responsible to my village of God by sharing faith lessons I learn from children and how they respond to my friendship offer in the name of Christ. As a pebble tossed into a pond makes ripples affecting the whole, so will my actions have unpredictable effect upon all humankind.

> Even as I remember persons who enriched my life as a child, I want to take my turn. Help me share the joys of this work done in the name of Christ. Make it a holy contagion to other adults so the work is multiplied thousands of times by adults serving children for the cause of Christ.

When a few thousand believers start such a holy revolution of love, it will spread like an uncontrolled prairie fire. It doesn't take much gifting, talent, boldness, or money to start—just a few people in a village of God doing deeds of kindness to children in the name of Jesus. Think how quickly a large number of people may be affected. The hard/easy work is to mirror the life of the Master and follow the apostle Paul's admonition, "Imitate me, just as I also imitate Christ" (1 Cor. 11:1).

A village of God can be where you are, and you can start it. The children you serve may be in your family, on your block, in your neighborhood, across town, or down the freeway. But they need you, and you need the holy fulfillment that comes from trying. Start by yourself if you can't find anyone to join you. Share the idea with your Bible study group or your prayer circle. Ask children's Sunday school teachers in your church to help you identify the child God wants you to help. If you're a pastor or lay leader in your church, why not consider refocusing part of your church's ministry on children? Children must experience the love of Christ just as they must have healthy food and learn their spelling and math.

One recent new believer in Christ, a young husband and father, said, "When someone loved our children, we knew the person was going to love us, too." That's why the couple turned to Christ—because they needed love for their children and for themselves. Only the people of God can make it happen in thousands of settings through villages of grace—churches, parachurch organizations, Bible study groups, prayer groups, and Christ-indwelt neighbors.

The challenge and the results are stated so beautifully and accurately on a plaque that appeared in a home decorating catalog: "A hundred years from now, it will not matter what my bank account was, the sort of house I lived in, or the kind of car I drove . . . but the world may be different because I was important in the life of a child."[12] You make the world better when you introduce a child to Christ.

How One Church Is Recovering the Village of Grace

Consider this incredible first-person report written by Pastor Aron P. Willis, senior pastor of High Point (North Carolina) First Wesleyan Church:

I am the senior pastor of a church campus which includes a multi-staffed congregation, a nursing home/retirement community, and a child care/Christian Academy (K–12). Because of growth and increasing demands for services, for the past two years church leaders had sought ways to accommodate the growth of campus ministries. Through the providence of God, a vacated shopping mall, consisting of 352,000 square feet, situated on 52 acres was made available to us.

However, as we moved through the laborious and demanding process of purchasing the property, the Lord took me through a season of brokenness. Initially, I feared the pressures of my work were shoving me to the brink of emotional collapse.

It was no coincidence that during this time of brokenness, the Holy Spirit had begun showing me areas in which I was spiritually defunct. Conviction led to confession. I repented of my shallow devotional life. Additionally, I stood before my congregation and repented of attitudinal sins. Here's the problem—my dream for purchasing a mall had been self-serving. The objective was to expand "our" ministries to reach more people like "us" so that "we" could continue authenticating our success story. But God began to show me the countless number of families outside the church and the growing number inside the church being battered and broken by the insidious war being waged against families. Other than denouncing the evils undermining family strength and deploring the casualties, as a pastor I had done little to help my church develop proactive ministries for hurting families.

With spiritual renewal, God gave me and our church leadership a vision for creating a family "wellness" center. We named the mall "Providence Place" and determined that it will be a center dedicated to the task of restoring, stabilizing, and enriching families, using a biblical and redemptive focus. Our strategy will be to bring together as many Christian services as possible for addressing family needs.

Some of the ministries we envision include a consortium of counseling services for resourcing and healing every dimension of family life, domestic abuse recovery, women's shelter, housing for unwed mothers (with transitional employment in retirement/nursing center), Crisis Pregnancy Center, adoption agency, foster home placement services, marriage enrichment workshops, career assessment services, financial planning, credit union, senior care and child care for serving the immediate community, a community youth center complete with recreational and study/mentoring areas.

Our fervent prayer is that God will use Providence Place, not only to restore and strengthen families in our area, but also to make it a prototype for other family wellness centers across our nation. We at High Point First Wesleyan Church in North Carolina are deeply humbled by the vision God has given us. Despite the enormous destabilization of families in recent years, we are convinced that the church, through the transforming power of Jesus Christ, can make a difference.

What Pattern Can You Use to Start a Village of Grace?

Providence Place uniquely fits the High Point church even as it challenges their people and financial resources.

Notice, however, their pattern started with spiritual motivation and brokenness connected to the pressing nearby needs of real people and specific families. That's the starting point for all of us—to care in the name of Jesus for nearby children and their families.

NOTES

1. Hillary Rodham Clinton, *It Takes a Village* (New York: Simon & Schuster, 1996), 16.

2. Jim Burton, *Home Life,* October 1995, 24–28.

3. Kay C. James, "Transforming America," *Imprints* (Hillsdale College, Hillsdale, Michigan), 1996, 2.

4. As quoted by James, ibid.

5. Ibid.

6. As quoted in *Current Thoughts & Trends,* April 1996, 9.

7. William Raspberry, "Politicians Can't Fix Our Problems—But We Can," *Gazette Telegraph* (Colorado Springs), April 23, 1996.

8. Summary of John Dilulio, "Kids Who Scare Cops," *Citizen,* January 15, 1996, cited in *Current Thoughts & Trends,* March 1996, 27.

9. Ibid.

10. Ibid.

11. As quoted by E. Glenn Wagner, *The Awesome Power of Shared Beliefs* (Waco: Word, 1995), 56.

12. *Paragon* catalog, spring–summer 1996.

PART 2
THE AMAZING POWER OF THE FAMILY OF GOD

Chapter 6

FAMILY OF GOD ACCORDING TO SCRIPTURE

Developing the Biblical Pattern

The family was God's idea, and it came into being at creation. Scripture frequently uses family words to describe relationships between biblical characters.

The family of God is delightful to experience but difficult to define. The family of God is a relationship and a loving place to belong. It's a connection with supportive brothers and sisters committed to Christ, which enables and encourages healthy, intangible strengths such as trust, honesty, love, loyalty, belonging, and forgiveness. It's a place to be loved and a supportive association with like-minded people. It's a spiritual home significantly better than Robert Frost's idea: "Home is the place where, when you have to go there, they have to take you in."[1]

Though the phrase "family of God" does not appear often in the Bible, family concepts permeate the whole of Scripture. Consider these two powerful biblical references: "For this reason I bow my knees to the Father of our Lord Jesus Christ, from whom *the whole family* in heaven and earth is named" (Eph. 3:14–15, italics added), and "Let us not grow weary while doing good, for in due season we shall reap if we do not lose heart. Therefore, as we have opportunity, let us do good to all, especially to those *who are of the household of faith"* (Gal. 6:9–10, italics added). That's authentic family talk—to bear God's name and to be charged with doing good to the family of believers. The Bible speaks of Jesus' relationships to His earthly kin, to His adopted spiritual family composed of His disciples, and to His extended family of followers consisting of all who do God's will. The fatherhood of God is mentioned frequently, along with our relationship to the Father as His sons and daughters. Then, too, Jesus extols childlikeness as a worthy pattern for serving Him and others.

The familylike characteristics found in so many places in the Bible motivate us to find ways to reenergize the family of God, especially for children. Halford Luccock's comments concerning Acts 1:13 inspire a new appreciation for the tender bonds the family of God stands ready to provide us. The passage reads, "Peter, James, John, and Andrew; Philip and Thomas; Bartholomew and Matthew; James the son of Alphaeus and Simon the Zealot; and Judas the son of James." Though the verse at first sounds uninspiring, Luccock draws a helpful perspective on family from the passage:

> Listen to the roll call in the upper room at Jerusalem, as we catch echoes of it in the thirteenth verse of the first chapter of Acts. Then consider this thought: take away four families from this first Christian church and what do you have left? . . . Here was the Zebedee family with James and John on the official board. Here was another family with the brothers Peter and Andrew. Here were some of Jesus' own family. It is a perfect picture of what most churches are. Here are the Joneses, the Browns, the Robinsons, and the Smiths. Just a family church but as such it follows the original pattern of

the most tremendous force in history. Christianity found its most transforming influence in primary human institutions. The family church has a great inheritance. It should lift itself up to a new sense of worth and importance. What did Jesus leave to the world? Much in every way. But high among His greatest legacies was this—He left a family church.[2]

There's that combination of the family and the church again that follows us throughout so much of Scripture—the family of God that Luccock calls "the original pattern of the most tremendous force in history." What a force it is, and how badly we need that force in our society now.

Think what the family of God can mean for contemporary people. Think what it meant for ancient people. Imagine our fascination when we (H. B. and Neil) read a single commentary about the two Scriptures from Paul mentioned earlier. In ten or twelve pages, we found this random list of traits of God's family—the church:

- A place of instruction and example
- A relationship to the Father God and our spiritual siblings
- A place where God's children are disciplined to make us holy
- A relationship of protection, security, and safety
- A place where the everlasting God is Father of the family
- A relationship where everyone belongs to a big eternal family
- A place where we receive support when pain and grief come
- A relationship where fellow believers stick closer than brothers or sisters

- A place where every relationship is rooted in God
- A relationship where everyone bears the family name—Christian
- A relationship of affirming affection

What a list of assuring realities. No wonder so many love the family of God so much. Rejoice in these wonderful relationships and search for effective ways to share them with children you know. Think of the benefits for millions of kids who live their whole lives in terrible despair.

We Teach Children About a Nearby God

But can children really understand God's message? Yes— even very young children. Sammy was four and a half years old. His parents had been having severe problems. There were lots of fighting and hurting each other. Because of that, Sammy was often afraid.

One day, Sammy told a grown-up friend about being afraid. The friend told him this: "Sammy, Jesus is with you all the time. He's with you when you're afraid. Jesus has said, 'I will never leave you.' The next time you're afraid, talk to Jesus about it. Say, 'Dear Jesus, please help me.' "

A few days later, Sammy was with his friend again. The friend asked, "Who is always with you, Sammy?" "Jesus," answered Sammy. "And what does Jesus say to us?" "I will never leave you." "What should you do when you're afraid?" "Say, 'Dear Jesus, please help me.' "

Children can be taught to have such a close relationship with a caring God, and it makes a big difference in the problems they face.

God's Family Likeness in the Church

Though family specialist Paul Pearsall was not discussing the church, his powerful sentence about secular families shines a spotlight on the possibilities of the family of God: "Being part of any family can be the most important privilege of being human, the most healing experience of being alive, and the source of a lifelong and evolving understanding of what it really means to live."[3] Think what it means to a little boy to be told, "You act like your father." Think how special a Christian feels to be told, "You love children like your Father does."

The twofold message of the Bible to the contemporary church is (1) to become an extended family for every child and (2) to teach nonfragmented families how to develop and strengthen their biological families. Individuals, society, and the nation desperately need contemporary churches to immediately pursue these two equally important goals with vigor and commitment.

One family specialist said, "Families are not failing, but we are failing families."[4] He is right, and that means more contemporary churches need to do more *familying*— strengthening family members, welcoming new infants in Christ to the inner life of the church, happily making room for and accepting unattached persons who do not have natural family, and helping everyone with parenting, grandparenting, and extended family skills and strategies. At its best, the church becomes like a wholesome family that gives and receives love to everyone it touches. Such a bonding of affection and acceptance shows on nearly every page of the Bible.

Scriptural Principles About the Family of God

The Bible helps us see that just as children are of supreme importance to God, so they must be important to us. We must love children and cherish them and train them and develop them because God wants all of these things to happen. And God expects the church to lead in this adventuresome task. Let's explore ten scriptural principles that help us maximize the universal strength the family of God can provide for our children.

Principle 1: God Created the Family (Gen. 1:27–28)

According to the creation record, God created families from the dust of the ground. Teaching about family soon followed in the first chapter of Genesis: "So God created man in His own image; in the image of God He created him; male and female He created them. Then God blessed them, and God said to them, 'Be fruitful and multiply; fill the earth and subdue it; have dominion over the fish of the sea, over the birds of the air, and over every living thing that moves on the earth'" (vv. 27–28). The placing of human beings into families started with God at creation. Since He created us for relationships, those who do not live in families miss something significant.

Children are created by God in His image, with potential for becoming vital persons in His kingdom. Listen in holy awe to Psalm 139:13–15:

For You formed my inward parts;
You covered me in my mother's womb.
I will praise You, for I am fearfully and wonderfully made;
Marvelous are Your works,

And that my soul knows very well.
My frame was not hidden from You,
When I was made in secret,
And skillfully wrought in the lowest parts of the earth.

Principle 2: Everyone Is Welcome in God's Family (John 1:12–13)

Scripture supports this idea in many settings. One incredibly clear promise announces, "As many as received Him, to them He gave the right to become children of God, to those who believe in His name: who were born, not of blood, nor of the will of the flesh, nor of the will of man, but of God" (John 1:12–13). All believers are part of a holy family where God welcomes them as His children. Membership in His family leads to significance and a purposeful life. Christ promises the best quality life ever discovered by the whole human race.

Principle 3: God's Family Lives by Love (John 13:34–35)

Love is the main family trait in God's family. He requires love from His family. He provides love for His family. He empowers His family to love one another.

Here's the charge to love given by our Lord, "A new commandment I give to you, that you love one another; as I have loved you, that you also love one another. By this all will know that you are My disciples, if you have love for one another" (John 13:34–35).

Even healthy human families discover deepening affection for one another when they follow the teachings of Christ. Even when natural families are broken, their hurting and pained members can find acceptance and affirmation in God's family. Our love to God and God's love to us make every authentic disciple more loving to everyone else. That includes the family of God, the biological family, the neighbors, and the world.

At the heart of the Christian gospel is an inclusive community of persons who care for one another, who care for needy persons around them. It's a fulfilling way to live and a blessed bonded relationship to build, cultivate, and receive. And it's a grand place to raise children.

Principle 4: God's Love Reaches Across Generations (Deut. 7:9)

What wonderful assurance we have to know God keeps working across years and across generations. Our Father is the One who "keeps covenant and mercy for a thousand generations with those who love Him and keep His commandments" (Deut. 7:9). Think how long a thousand generations must be. His faithfulness works longer than we can imagine in the lives of those who have no idea God is answering the prayers of earlier generations in them.

Notice how Scripture joins "covenant" and "mercy" in this passage. Covenants are legal documents that produce legal obligations. They are to be legally implemented and followed; both parties keep covenants because that is expected of them. But when Scripture puts love and covenant together, you can be absolutely sure of God's love reaching to you and to a thousand generations of people yet unborn.

Principle 5: In the Family of God, Restoration Is Always Possible (Gal. 4:4–7)

In Jesus Christ, God came into the world in human form to make it possible for all people to be part of the Father's family. Paul explains clearly in his Galatian letter: "But when the fullness of the time had come, God sent forth His

Son, born of a woman, born under the law, to redeem those who were under the law, that we might receive the adoption as sons. And because you are sons, God has sent forth the Spirit of His Son into your hearts, crying out, 'Abba, Father!' Therefore you are no longer a slave but a son, and if a son, then an heir of God through Christ" (Gal. 4:4–7).

These words carry mind-boggling truth—we are no longer slaves because we have been adopted as sons and daughters; we have full family rights and privileges. Since we live in holy, empowering relationship, God has made us heirs to the family resources and riches. Think of the implications for now and forever. Think how many fatherless children will delight to hear that good news.

Principle 6: The Family of God Goes Beyond Bloodlines (Matt. 12:46–50)

Scripture reminds us from the life of Christ,

> While He was still talking to the multitudes, behold, His mother and brothers stood outside, seeking to speak with Him. Then one said to Him, "Look, Your mother and Your brothers are standing outside, seeking to speak with You." But He answered and said to the one who told Him, "Who is My mother and who are My brothers?" And He stretched out His hand toward His disciples and said, "Here are My mother and My brothers! For whoever does the will of My Father in heaven is My brother and sister and mother" (Matt. 12:46–50).

That is an incredible word of grace to all who do the will of God. Count on the promise—you are a member of the family of Jesus if you do the will of the Father.

Principle 7: God Wants His Family to Meet Human Need (James 2:14–17)

The apostle James summarized this idea that appears in several biblical passages: "What does it profit, my brethren, if someone says he has faith but does not have works? Can faith save him? If a brother or sister is naked and destitute of daily food, and one of you says to them, 'Depart in peace, be warmed and filled,' but you do not give them the things which are needed for the body, what does it profit? Thus also faith by itself, if it does not have works, is dead" (James 2:14–17). Try thinking through the implications of that passage in our time for helping the bruised and beat-up and broken children. Surely, every contemporary congregation has responsibility for children of all ages. Surely, the passage has a component of caring for children who have been spiritually and emotionally scarred by divorce, desertion, or despair.

Principle 8: The Family of God Prospers When Faith Is Taught and Caught (Deut. 6:5–9)

Living as a Christian is always harder when one is isolated from the family of faith with its tender love and happy associations. That's why John Wesley taught there is no such thing as solitary religion. It is in relationships that this faith is to be lived and learned and expressed in love.

A representative biblical teaching about this idea can be found in the instructions recorded in Deuteronomy:

> You shall love the LORD your God with all your heart, with all your soul, and with all your strength. And these words which I command you today shall be in your heart. You shall teach them diligently to your children, and shall talk of them when

you sit in your house, when you walk by the way, when you lie down, and when you rise up. You shall bind them as a sign on your hand, and they shall be as frontlets between your eyes. You shall write them on the doorposts of your house and on your gates (6:5–9).

That sounds as if we are to constantly cultivate an awareness of the goodness of God and His bountiful provision for the human family and for the family of God.

Without pushing the passage to make it say more than it means, this Scripture appears to call us to live in ways that attract children—ours and others'—to God. The passage calls us to show young people how faith works in the family and the home.

An idea here is often overlooked—those who teach the truth to children are helped as much by telling and retelling as the children who hear. A ninety-year-old woman told us her worship experiences were changed forever when she taught a lesson to third graders years ago about how the ancient scribes were so awed by God that they always stopped to wash their pens before writing God's name in their manuscripts. What you teach children sometimes does something great to you.

Principle 9: The Family of God Thrives When It Gives Itself for Others (Matt. 25:40)

The family of God has always been a caring group who could not be satisfied to see anyone in need of any kind. The early church learned to give itself rich by responding to every need it encountered. That lesson must be relearned in every generation—giving makes the church richer, never poorer.

The contemporary family of God can't be satisfied to simply discuss the incredible problems of children in our society. It's time to act. No more shaking our heads in surprise at what sin does to our kids; it's time to move beyond dialogue to decisions. It's time to stop debating and start doing. Doing means caring. Caring means giving. Giving means making a difference. Action that produces life-changing achievement is needed now. All this means opening our hearts, our resources, and our actions to children.

The family of God cares for and nurtures children because Jesus did. The church ministers to children because doing so is right. It develops children because the future of the world and the church depends on it. It loves children because a God-inspired pull in its heart motivates it to do so.

Throughout Christian history, the family of God has had few rivals in nurturing children. Wherever the church has gone, it has ministered to the bodies and minds and souls of children even as it has pointed them to Christ.

What has been done for children in developing countries and what has been done for hundreds of years in mission settings must be replicated today in Western society, especially in urban settings. That's among our most urgent tasks.

Principle 10: The Family of God Develops People (2 Cor. 3:18—4:1)

We can rejoice to recall that those who bear the family name Christian are always family, and God is shaping all of His family into Christlikeness. God has put the church in the human potential development business. That means everyone, including unconventional uncles, noisy brothers, selfish sisters, sassy cousins, and stingy granddads. One little boy explained about his teen sister, "She's a pain in the neck, but she's our pain in the neck." Children in every neighborhood need the family of God to treat them as family even if they are "our pain in the neck."

Hear the good news about potential development—our own and that of others: "But we all, with unveiled face, beholding as in a mirror the glory of the Lord, are being transformed into the same image from glory to glory, just as by the Spirit of the Lord. Therefore, since we have this ministry, as we have received mercy, we do not lose heart" (2 Cor. 3:18—4:1).

All children need a church to accept and love them even when they are not so lovable. Such acceptance sometimes takes hard work, but the payoff can be absolutely amazing and unbelievably incredible.

Both payoff and accountability from serving children are stated almost poetically in Richard Lischer's comment about Martin Luther King's childhood: "At Ebenezer Baptist Church, young King learned that when the preacher assumes his proper place in the hierarchy above the people and beneath the cross—and says what God wants him to say—the entire organism hums with power. The people had better pay attention."[5] King probably would never have been heard of without the shaping influence of the church. That reality is true for thousands of others who have shaped society throughout the centuries of the Christian church.

Are You Ready to Apply Scripture to Yourself As You Work with Big Mart?

So far in this chapter and others, we have almost insinuated that the children we are called to serve are sweet, though neglected little children the church should help. That is exactly right for some, but not true for others. Some children have turned to violence because that's all they know. Some have turned to gangs because they do not have anyone else to accept them. Some will try our souls and make us want to give up. But when all the issues and possibilities are added up, we need energy and courage to keep trying. It can be wonderful and terrible at the same time.

We want to share a story that Don Bakely tells about his ministry in a changing neighborhood in New Jersey. It's about Big Mart and Ella. It seems Bakely was called to serve a congregation of aging middle-class people whose church was located in a changing neighborhood. The church had lost all contact with its neighborhood, especially teens and kids. So Bakely made contact with the neighborhood gang, talked with them, even wrestled with them, and finally got them to attend church occasionally.

The first day Big Mart (his real name was Marshall) came into the church, he had a big disagreement with the church secretary and called her by a dirty, foul name. Ella was the church secretary and the reigning matriarch of the congregation all wrapped into one person. When Mart insulted her, Ella marched into the pastor's office and demanded, "What are you going to do with that gang member outside in my office?"

Pastor Bakely responded, "That's a good question. But the more pressing issue is, what are you going to do about it?"

She said, "I want you to throw him out now."

"Ella," the pastor said, "I've been working for six weeks to get Mart in here. I just can't throw him out until you have at least heard his story."

"Tell me," she replied.

Here's the story behind the story: "When Big Mart was a small boy, his father came home one night and beat his mother to death. He was so violent he insisted the children watch him kill the mother. After the murder, the father cut her head off in front of the children. That's right—he made them watch. When Big Mart could stand no more, he ran for the door and started down the steps of their apartment building. His father became so enraged that he threw the mother's head on Big Mart and knocked him down the steps. He's the same guy who called you that bad name, Ella."

Ella left the room, and the pastor didn't know what to say or think. Finally, in about twenty minutes, she returned. Neither the pastor nor Ella could find a way to restart the conversation. Finally, Ella said, "I guess I'll just have to learn how to be called bad names."

Bakely closes the story with a powerful sentence: "That's the day that church began ministry to its neighborhood youth."[6] We thank God for Ella's and Pastor Bakely's courage and perspective. Big Mart will finally find his way to Christ because of them.

Though you may never meet a Big Mart in your area, there are children and teens who have never been loved. There are children who know nothing about God. In every setting, there are children who will be secularized on the outside and empty on the inside if a church doesn't reach them and their families and do it soon.

Look around you in any direction to see children who need a church to love them, a Sunday school to teach them, a family to cherish them, and a Christ-centered group to accept them. Their future depends on it, the future of the nation depends on it, and the future viability of the church depends on it.

It takes a church to make a difference for kids. Years ago,

Yakov Smirnoff, a Russian comedian, brought all of this into focus when he told a reporter,

> My mother told me a story when I was a child. When Leo Tolstoy was an old man, he was planting little apple trees. His neighbor laughed at him and called him a silly old man, because when the apples finally grew he wouldn't be around to eat them. Tolstoy replied, "Yes, but other people will eat them and they will think of me." I think that's what we're supposed to do: Leave more than we've found, give more than we've received, love more than we've been loved.[7]

His words sound like Jesus' loving, though demanding, words in Scripture, "Whoever receives one of these little children in My name receives Me" (Mark 9:37). In our relationships with children, the challenge is to love more than we've been loved, give more than we have been given, and leave more than we found.

NOTES

1. Robert Frost, "The Death of a Hired Man," as quoted in *Bartlett's Familiar Quotations* (Boston: Little, Brown, 1980), 747.

2. Halford Luccock, *The Acts of the Apostles* (New York: Willett, Clark, 1938), 28–29.

3. Paul Pearsall, *Power of the Family* (New York: Bantam, 1990), 4.

4. Ibid.

5. Richard Lischer, *The Preacher King* (New York: Oxford Press, 1995), 22.

6. Adapted from *Hard Living People and Main Stream Christians* by Tex Sample. Copyright © 1993 by Abingdon Press. Used by permission.

7. As quoted by David Friend and the editors of *Life, The Meaning of Life* (Boston: Little, Brown, 1991), 174.

Chapter 7

ENERGIZING THE PARTNERSHIP

Foundations for Stronger Homes

THIEF STEALS HOME! shouts the headline. The California newspaper story tells about a house mover who put a home up on timbers and moved it during the night to avoid traffic snarls. The house was stored on a giant house-moving trailer next to a large hole where a foundation was soon to be built. But before the foundation was finished, someone attached a big truck to the trailer and stole the house.

That true story forms a parable for this chapter. A home without a church is like a house without a foundation. The church and the family naturally belong together to provide strength and support to each other. Neither can make it without the other. The church, like no other institution, is in the best position to either prevent or solve our problems with children and their families. But will it?

Siamese Twins Belong Together

Family specialist Charles Sell encourages us to an all-out effort to renew and strengthen this partnership: "The Christian church and the Christian home are as closely bonded together as Siamese twins. If they are cut apart, a major artery may be severed that causes one or both to hemorrhage or die."[1] Think of the connections between church and home. Think of the dependencies where one supports and reinforces the other.

God formed the biological family at creation and established the family of God, the church, on the day of Pentecost. Throughout Scripture and history, God gives incredible priority to the church and the family in His plans for humankind. The Father intends for church and family to fortify, augment, and complement each other.

Dr. James Dobson explains the necessity of keeping this relationship healthy:

> Only two bulwarks of the Judeo-Christian ethic remain, and they both face unrelenting pressures. The first is the Christian church, which has been on the defensive in recent years and has lost its taste for battle. . . . The second repository of Judeo-Christian values is the institution of the family. Alas, the beleaguered, exhausted, oppressed, and overtaxed family now stands unprotected against a mighty foe. If it collapses, and if the church fails to mobilize, the Civil War could be over in a matter of days.[2]

If we are to give the next generation a healthy spiritual future, the family and the church must be revitalized and mobilized. What appears bleak can be made bright.

The Challenge Could Strengthen Us

When either the biological or the church family is depreciated, we fail to account for centuries of strength and influence. Millions cherished the family and the church as dear treasures that gave them a reason for being.

Building on these interdependent strengths, author Larry Richards asks a demanding question dealing with the heart of the partnership between church and family, "Are we willing to do what must be done so the church can help the family face the future?"[3] That's the issue facing every contemporary church: Is it willing to do that?

After considering alternatives, we soon realize we have no choice. Without the church, the family does not have much of a future. Neither does the church have much future without the family. Every person needs the family and the church to have a healthy and viable future. Society needs everything the family and the church represent to be strong and vigorous and righteous.

However, the task of bringing the church and the home into a viable partnership is too big for mere human effort. Let us explain with a story. A member of the Chicago Bulls basketball team was once asked about his most memorable experience in playing on the same team with Michael Jordan. His response: "Oh, the night Michael Jordan and I scored seventy points!" What he didn't say was that Michael Jordan scored sixty-nine of those points and he scored only one. That is the way our work is in family ministry. We represent one basket, but God provides sixty-nine; and we always win when we are in partnership with our Father.

In our time, neither the home nor the church is as hale and hardy as we wish it were. As significant influences in our society, the church and the family are being attacked on many fronts while being ignored on others. Politicians speak of the family in meaningless rhetoric because everyone lives in a family or came from a family or both; thus, vote-getting expediency motivates them to talk about family without offering much substance. Even longtime friends of the church and the home often have second thoughts about both. And the depressing statistics about children alarm everyone. These are not good times for the church or the family. But both are needed too much for us to allow them to become feeble or anemic.

Meanwhile, Scripture, clearly in sync with human experience, insists the church and the family are necessary for individuals and for the common good. If the church and the family disappeared from the face of the earth, God or human beings would have to create something like them immediately because they are essential for human wholeness. Amazing but true—the moment when church and family are being bashed so thoroughly is the precise time when they are needed more than ever.

We must resuscitate and revitalize the family and the church. Why look for other villages to save our children when the only remaining characteristics of a village are contained in the family and the church? For too long we have mistakenly expected schools, communities, and government to solve children's problems, but they don't—and can't— and won't.

Everybody Needs Relationships

The people of God, along with most of our society, lost something incredibly valuable when we started to give up on the church and the family. Something was lost that is as vital to our souls as food is to our bodies. Think of it—without murmuring or protesting, we allowed secular forces to steal the foundation of the family and the church while we flirted with the possibility we could make it without them. It was a grievous error that has to be corrected.

Now we know better. Now we know how much we need family. Now we realize a visceral killer called loneliness has infected millions. Yesterday I (Neil) saw it in the eyes of people on the streets, at a fast-food restaurant, in the next car at a traffic stoplight, and at the airport. Today I saw it in the eyes of a neighbor and a UPS delivery man. I heard it, too, on outrageous afternoon TV talk shows, at the supermarket checkout counter, and in a Sunday school class. I even heard it at a debate between a street preacher and an avowed atheist on Leicester Square in London—both needed someone like a family or a church to care for them and love them.

You can observe intense isolation in children, too. Watch them when they try to talk to a friendly adult stranger in a department store or when they try to make friends with another child at the day care center or at Little League practice.

Human beings, especially children, were created for relationships. Without tender human ties, we all shrivel emotionally and spiritually. From personal experience, we know we will become emotionally and spiritually ill if we have no group where we belong, no group where we feel accepted, and no group where we are held accountable. I (H. B.) often say that everyone needs a team to play on, a choir to sing in, and a group to belong to. Millions seek what has always been a specialty of the church in all the wrong places. God intends for the church to be what a lonely man said to the church where he worshiped, "You are the family I never had, and I love you for it."

The Church and the Family Must Be Revived

As so often happens when something significant starts to decline, we report how bad things are rather than how good they could be with a little corrective effort. That is what is happening with the family and the church bashing in our society. Let's try to understand just how much our children actually lose when the family and the church are being ignored or are in decline. We cannot afford to lose love, spirituality, accountability, affirmation, relationship, loyalty, obligation, and stability. And though some may argue these factors can be found in other relationships, they are not being experienced in very large measure anywhere these days.

Let's acknowledge family forms are changing rapidly. Charles Sell explains the realities we must factor into our awareness of the situation:

> What Americans thirty years ago thought as the typical family is no longer the majority. Then typical meant a family with a husband who was the provider, a wife who was the homemaker, and several children. In 1960, 60 percent of all households were like that, now, only 7 percent are. Even if we add families with one or more children in which both the husband and wife work outside the home, it still adds up to only 26.7 percent of households in the U.S. . . . Yet with all these changes, most people still grow up in a family and live with relatives. Family households (where two or more related people live) far outnumber non-family households (persons living alone or with a non-relative) by 70.2 percent to 29.8 percent. The norm is still for people to marry (over 90 percent of adults do) and bear children in a family context. So, in a sense, some form of the traditional family is still very much present.[4]

Obviously, things are not the way they were even two or three decades ago, but that does not mean we can give up. Sell continues, "Fifty-eight percent of married women with children under six years of age are in the labor force. . . .

Similarly the rate of married women working who have children ages 6–17 has increased from 49 percent twenty years ago to 73 percent today."[5] Families are changed, never to be as they were. But that means the church is even more needed now.

Facing these realities—even the unfriendly ones—the church is still obligated to help families and children be truly Christian as they live immersed in the new realities. Thus our call for a renewed partnership between home and church is a challenge to move forward to what can be in this new era. This may be a grand time for the church to renew commitments to provide acceptance, assimilation, and a sense of belonging for everyone, especially children.

Our new era is something like the period in American history when the church was forced to move from the country to town as people left farms. The church had to be nearer the people, to be scheduled differently, to empower them to build new relationships, and to address new stress points. For the church, the move from farm to town required new strategies for delivering the gospel to the people. Though the situation did not change the message, it did require different methods in its new settings.

Curse the Darkness or Light a Candle?

We must ask ourselves, Can the church minister to the new diversities of family forms and still be the church? Can the church continue to be the church while ignoring changes in the family? In times like these, a church has to ask, What is acceptable and what is destructive? What is tolerable even though it is not ideal?

Changes in family life have already had tremendous impact on churches. Two examples are single parents and working moms; they have revolutionized and diminished every church's voluntary workforce. Now there are more children to serve from church families with fewer volunteers, and there are significantly fewer volunteers to serve children who come from unchurched homes.

In this whole process of serving Christ during a social revolution, churches will be forced to evaluate modifications of traditional families and respond to the changes the way they think Christ would respond. These reevaluations are far-reaching and will likely include issues such as priority of expenditures, the moral standing of unmarried couples living together, sermons about marriage when singles are present, urban churches serving children in poverty, cultural minorities, Christian grandparenting, and unacceptable divorce.

The new questions keep coming: How can a church be redemptive without moral compromise? How can a church be forgiving without becoming permissive? What can be done to spark spiritual reformation in people who are caught up in moral despair? How much brokenness in people's past can a church accept while preaching a holistic gospel that keeps attracting hurting people like a holy magnet? And how willing is the church to go into the ghettos of society to rescue millions of hurting children?

After all these questions are answered, we must face the fact that the family of God is the only family many people will ever have. To be true to itself, the Lord, and its mission, the church must go to work. The church has a sacred responsibility to salt a decaying society with Christ's good news. And while we must be cautious about thinking a church can ever be a substitute for biological families, that's the reality for many of today's children. We must strengthen the human family, but when it can't be strengthened, the family of God has to do what it can. Children, regardless of the circumstances of their birth or their living conditions, must be shown in every possible way that Christ has a better way for them than they sometimes see at home.

Maximizing the Power of the Partnership

This partnership is a three-way alliance between the biological family, the church family, and God—the heavenly Father. God is the senior member of this family partnership. As with all our efforts in family and church, we depend on His enablement and grace to be what we can be and to become what He wants us to become. Let's consider several ways to strengthen this relationship.

This Partnership Builds Churches by Validating a Church's Reason for Being

Too many churches in North America have a foggy mission. Thousands of people meet at church each week to do what they have always done and go home satisfied that they have done their duty for another week. But in this frightening epidemic of children's problems, every church is touched by these concerns in some way, whether in the country, town, suburbs, or city. Ignoring them will not make them go away.

Offering ministry to people with needs is a common perspective for shaping ministry that attracts and excites both those who receive ministry and those who give ministry. By renewing the church, we mean a new vision, a new impact on a community, and a new concern for those in the fellowship who face these problems. We mean a new commitment to serve every family who is open to the gospel on the assumption that all parents have some concern about whether they are going to be able to effectively raise their children—to hold a newborn baby for the first time is to become aware of a responsibility that will not go away for at least twenty years, and will probably be with you all the days of your life.

This idea of renewing the church or giving it higher visibility in the community shines through the story of George Spencer, who went to a small Oregon coastal town to plant a church about ten years ago. He went there without one contact, only with the assurance from God that he was to go. For six months he worked as a bag boy in the only grocery store in town. That way he made contacts with many young families. Soon George, his wife, and their children started an after-school boys' and girls' club program on Tuesdays in their family room. The group grew, so they started a similar group on Monday. Then another group on Wednesday afternoon. Then another on Thursday and finally one on Friday.

By that time, they had enough family contacts to think about starting a church, so they did. About three years after the church was started, a reporter asked five or six families why they were a part of the new church that had no facilities, little money, and no seasoned reputation. Almost in unison, they replied, "We're worried about our kids having right influences. When George showed our children love, it was natural to start loving him in return."

Could it be that serious commitments to children in every church would create a new curiosity about the church and its potential importance in people's lives? A veteran country preacher used to tell beginning pastors, "When you care for the children, the whole extended family will show interest."

Even folks who say the church is irrelevant, unconcerned with real issues, too self-serving, or has nothing important to say to contemporary people are forced to listen when a church serves their children in the name of Christ. A children-sensitive church will grow in influence and attendance.

This Partnership Provides Faith Resources to Parents

Parenting is a task for which people have little training. It never fails that when I buy a car, the salesperson gives me more instructions about the automobile than anyone in our society gave me about parenting. To become whole persons, children need parents and other adults to feed them faith. But what parent knows how to do that naturally?

The church can offer parenting training to parents. Sometimes this training is done in a formal class setting. Other times it happens when a faithful believer shares his own discoveries about Christian parenting. Many of us have learned a lot about parenting by teaching children's Sunday school classes. And more progressive churches are now distributing books and pamphlets about Christian parenting.

Here's a first-person essay by a young woman who was raised in a church I (Neil) once pastored. The essay is entitled "God Called (with a Little Help)" and demonstrates how vital it is for a church to help persons be good parents:

How does God decide whom to call to do ministry? I can't answer for the rest of you, but I know how my call came about. One day (well it wasn't exactly a day, since they don't measure time in heaven), one moment in eternity, God was looking down on our church and realized that we were going to need a new director of religious education soon. Don't ask me how God knew this, He just did. So God called His counselors together, and they started looking over potential candidates to be God-called to this ministry. This is where my mother comes in.

My mother joined God in heaven a little over three years ago, when God knew it was time for her reward and I didn't know how much I still needed her here on earth. My mother was a reserved person and seldom stood up for herself or her needs. However, you could always count on my mother to stand up for her family.

My mother would never dream of considering herself one of God's counselors, but I image she did enjoy listening in on their discussions now and then since she was a curious person who took pleasure in learning new things. It is part of her heritage as a school teacher for many years. As Mom was listening at this moment in eternity, she heard my name mentioned, so she moved in closer to listen better. Someone was talking about my qualifications as a potential religious education director, and without hesitation, my mother stood up for her daughter. She declared, "Call her; she knows the stories." "She knows the stories?" "Yes," replied my mother, "when you teach children about God's love, you must be able to tell them the stories. Jesus told stories. She knows the stories!"

God must have chuckled at her insistence and maternal pride and asked Mom, "How can you be so sure she knows the stories?"

Her humble reply, "She knows the stories because I taught them to her."

I received the call, and I plan to fulfill it. Thanks, Mom, I love you.[6]

Every person who touched Wave Dreher or her mother, Bertha Beltz, had some small part in this faith development that moves across generational lines. Bertha learned the stories because someone told her in a church somewhere, and she sharpened them by telling them over and over to children in the churches where she taught Sunday school. And Bertha told them to her daughter at home.

The church multiplies its impact on children when it gives parents training and resources for faith development at home.

This Partnership Exhibits God's Love to a Community

This love is not theoretical because it has a human and divine face in Jesus Christ. The songwriter put our Lord's plan for us in poetic words: "They'll know we are Christians by our love." Nearly every problem children experience could be significantly lessened or eliminated by people demonstrating the love of God to them. As we wrote this book, a surprising number of believers suggested beautiful stories about how individuals in their past loved them to Christ when they were children—a love they are now passing on to other children. Jesus, of course, taught that loving another was a good gift we give ourselves because we are enriched when we give love and enriched again and again when love is returned in a thousand different ways.

Melissa tells a love story from her childhood. Alma was an adult who showed God's love to Cindy, an unchurched child like many children who live near every church.

Eight-year-old Melissa was sitting in her Sunday school class when a younger child, Cindy, was led into the room by her older sister. Melissa says,

> I could tell they were bus children from the poorer section of town because their clothes were messy and worn. Cindy was six years old. She loved music. She was from an abusive home. Her parents were "mean," and they never attended church. As a child, that was difficult for me to understand because I had never known anyone with abusive parents.

Cindy, her brother, and her two sisters came to church every week. They even began coming during the week with an older lady named Alma who lived just a few blocks from their home. Alma picked them up for church every time the doors opened. I think she wanted to get them into a loving environment as often as possible. Families with children near their ages would bring clothes for Cindy and her siblings to wear. . . . People donated money for camps and retreats—things Cindy and her brother and sisters can never afford.

Cindy continued to develop her love for music. The music leader at our church, Margaret, helped her prepare solos to present to the whole church. Someone gave her a flute, and she began to play as well as sing.

Cindy faithfully attended our church from the time she was six until she left for college. She was nurtured and encouraged by a church community to be the best that she could be in all she chose to do. As a teen, she accepted Christ. She earned extra money by serving as janitor of the church. She did well in extracurricular activities. During her teen years, she began to give back to the church through her care and teaching of other children.

The years have passed, and we lost contact until the church's 75th Anniversary Celebration. I had not seen Cindy for years. She attended the celebration from another town where she now lives with her husband and daughter. She is a nurse and a faithful member of her church.

The whole story came together for me when she sang a solo for the 75th celebration. Her song choice that day was "Love Will Be Your Home." The theme was exactly right because it was through love and the care of people at church that she found a spiritual home. The church became a place of safety, acceptance, and support where she could grow into the person God created her to be.[7]

Notice from this story what persons outside the church so often overlook. The church leads people to Christ, and that changes their lives for the better. Thus, it is not merely a religious belief that they embrace but a wholesome new way of living. They find friends. They see opportunities. They are often introduced to a Christian college. They discover a whole new way of living and acting. They become contributing citizens who otherwise might not have been. The love of Christ lifts people to higher levels of living and to ordering their lives by higher values. The positive outcomes are usually a thousand times more impressive than any changes government programs are able to produce—Christ changes character and that makes all the difference.

This Partnership Gives a Child a Sound Spiritual Perspective Even When Spiritual Resources Are Not Present at Home

The community of faith has a great track record for changing people one at a time. Some of the most effective Christians are those whom somebody loved to Christ without worrying about their home environment that could not be changed and about how sophisticated the church's programs might or might not be. Instead, they simply loved a child and left the results with the Lord. They had the idea— I must do what I can do and trust God to do what I cannot do.

Dr. Miriam Hall—veteran teacher, children's ministry denominational executive, and seminary professor—tells a story about David. She first met him in a Sunday school class when he was eight. In his class, he was a noticeable exception to the other children in his ragged jeans and scuffed tennis shoes. He was a handsome boy, but his smile was tentative and his eyes pain filled. When he spoke, he stammered and said, "Me do it," like a child much younger than his eight years. One day, his Sunday school teacher called at David's home where he found half a dozen teens and young adults in an environment of unbelievable filth and an immoral atmosphere. While both parents worked, David and his numerous brothers were left in the questionable care of an assortment of young uncles—most of whom were more interested in beer and girlfriends than in caring for boys.

Later the teacher discovered that a tragic fire had occurred while the children were home alone. In the fire, a baby died, and David was labeled the culprit because he had been playing with matches.

The story continues—and gets better. Dr. Hall reports,

Several years later when David was older, one of my seminary students was his Sunday school teacher and I went to observe the teaching. To my delight, I also observed a very different David. Instead of a shy, withdrawn, stuttering child, I now saw a bright-eyed, happy-feeling boy doing a Bible memory activity with the other children. As the other children called out the words of the verse, he located the correct word cards and arranged them in the right order. His backward speech was gone; he spoke normally for a child his age.

A few moments later, a visitor entered the class to check on who wanted tickets for an upcoming Royals game. All over the class, eager children shared their excitement.

"My dad's taking me," said one.

"I'm going with Dad and my uncle," chimed in another.

Something drew my attention to David. The light had gone out of his eyes and he hung his head. He had no one to take him. Slumped in his seat, he was once again the dejected boy of earlier days.

But his teacher quickly moved to David's side and put his arm around him. He spoke softly, but I could hear the words. "Don't worry, David. I'll get you a ticket and you can go to the game with me."

Instantly David's head raised again. The light returned to his eyes. Once again, he was a happy, confident boy because someone cared.[8]

Though no one can predict David's future, it is likely to be significantly better than it would have been had he not been introduced to that Sunday school class.

As we (Neil and H. B.) heard David's story, we felt we wanted to help that child. Though we are miles from David and will likely never meet him, our emotions are not too much different from those of many caring adults. People just like us are in your church, and they want to help, too. They may never be able to teach a Sunday school class or sing in the choir, but many will be willing to do something or give money to help children like David. They stand ready if you'll share the vision, the needs, and the names of those who need help.

This Partnership Gives Many People Opportunity to Change Children's Lives

Too often in our stories of faith, we hear of a Sunday school teacher or a Christian worker who dramatically affected a child for Christ. It seems that one person did a heroic act of faith that won the child and changed his or her life forever. In fact, most children who come to Christ are won through many different influences by many people. That's why we call the church the community of faith and the family of God—it often involves the combined efforts of many.

Consider Tricia's story of faith told by a friend of children, Mrs. B. Consider how many people contributed to it. This event took place when Tricia was eight. In a church service, Tricia asked Christ into her life, and a caring Sunday school teacher instructed her that faith was to be shared and not hoarded.

So she shared her faith, and her friends made fun of her. Tricia told Mrs. B., "I don't want to be a Christian anymore." Puzzled, Mrs. B. asked the reason. "Because my friends make fun of me. They think I am dumb to believe in Jesus, and they say bad words to me," Tricia replied.

But after discussing her feeling with Mrs. B., Tricia tried again. One day when one of her friends let fly a string of swear words, Tricia said, "You shouldn't say words like that."

Her friend replied, "I know. I wish I could stop, but I just can't."

"I know who can help you stop," responded Tricia. "I'll take you home and let my mother tell you about Christ." And that is what she did.[9]

Think of all the people who did something to influence Tricia and her friend. There were parents. The family of God helped resource them to live out their faith in their home before their children. Psychologists and educators tell us that the influence of the home environment and relationships with parents cannot be overestimated.

Then consider committed children's leaders at church.

They spent hours preparing materials to teach, praying for children, and visiting boys and girls in their homes.

Then there were the pastor and church lay leaders. The pastor even had times in the worship service when he prepared something special for children. He bent down to shake Tricia's hand and greet her personally as she left the church following the worship service. Along with the pastor, all those lay leaders on the administrative team had a part in the congregation's commitments to make the church friendly to children.

And don't forget Mrs. B. How easy it would have been for her to react in shock when Tricia said she didn't want to be a Christian anymore. Instead, Mrs. B. heard the confusion behind those words and helped a child understand faith more clearly.

This Partnership Can Change Someone's World

A caring relationship with a child can do what formal systems and government policies cannot do. Who can gauge the impact of hundreds of Sunday school teachers on the nation every Sunday? Who knows what child will be lifted to spiritual wholeness because of the efforts of a youth sponsor or caring mentor? Who knows how many are being attracted to a higher quality of life because they are being introduced one by one to Christ? Those who study history and those who have had experience serving Christ know one person's influence on another in the name of Christ cannot be measured. We do know the accumulated influence is awe-inspiring and immense and immeasurable.

The impact on a child of one or two persons is evident in Lois Mae's faith formation story. She calls it, "You Can Make a Difference":

My father left our family when my youngest brother was two months old. My mother, a woman of high morals and determined values, raised seven children by herself in the small town of Ada, Michigan. She sent us to Sunday school at that little country church through the early to mid-1960's. We each started attending as soon as the church would allow— which I guess was when we were old enough to climb on that big yellow bus, which was when we were about in kindergarten. My mother was a good woman but not a Christian. She did attend the special occasion services at a Baptist church.

I was a typical bus kid. I faithfully attended Sunday, always riding on that yellow bus.

I loved Sunday school and children's church, almost as much as I loved the bus ride to that little country church. I especially remember two special Sunday school teachers. Miss Land taught the kindergarten class in the tiny church kitchen, and Mrs. Harp taught the third- and fourth-grade class. It was in Mrs. Harp's class that I, a sensitive young girl, asked Jesus into my heart.

Then, like most typical bus kids whose parents are not won to Christ by the time the child finishes sixth grade, I stopped attending church. I entered my teen years with a spiritual foundation, but with little nurturing or spiritual encouragement.

As a high school senior, I attended Young Life meetings. This was the "in" and "cool" thing to do with my circle of high school friends. Young Life summer camp was the highlight of any Young Lifer. I attended summer camp in Colorado with my Young Life group. Adventuring outside my home state to the mountains of Colorado was the appeal. I wasn't even certain if this camp experience was a Christian event—like the church camp I went to from that little country church when I was a child.

Little did I know that Young Life Summer Camp would change my life forever. Near the end of the week, the camp speaker gave a passionate call to the cross of Christ. He then dismissed 200 high schoolers to 20 minutes of silence under the evening starlit Colorado sky. The only instruction was that we were not to talk to any fellow campers. We could talk—but we could talk to God only.

I did just that! I knew exactly what to do. The foundation laid in that little country church came back to me as clear as the sky above. I prayed a prayer for forgiveness on that August 12, 1973, night—recalling many Bible verses memorized at that little country church. I remembered that prayer of dedication in Mrs. Harp's Sunday school class. And the genuine, personal concern of Mrs. Harp. The teaching and influence of that little country church came back so clearly that life-changing night.

I have now been in the Lord's service for nearly 23 years. I am an ordained minister and credit the small country church and their children's Sunday school teachers for laying the foundation and influencing my spiritual life and development.

Recently, I went back where I met some of the old timers who remembered the Stanley children from the '60s. I had the privilege of chatting with Joe and Alice Smith. Joe was our faithful and friendly bus driver. Alice said she drove past our house on Honey Creek just the week before and said to the women with her, "I wonder what the Stanley girls are doing now?"

It was an experience I will always cherish as I shared with her my testimony of full-time service to Christ—thanks to the influence of a Baptist church and the love I experienced in those formative years. You can make a difference in a child's life just like they did and just like I am trying to do now.[10]

This Partnership Offers Many Benefits to Family and Church

There are many other benefits a ministry partnership between church and children provides. Here's a partial but exciting list:

- Ministry to children makes a church relevant to contemporary needs.
- Ministry to children helps society solve many of its largest failures. The generosity of American society to the needs of children has not solved those needs. New solutions are needed, and the raw materials for some solutions can be found only in the church.
- Ministry to children can be accomplished through the church without increased money or red tape because every congregation has experienced volunteers within its ranks. The church is made up of people who are experienced at child raising and experienced at Christian service. What a magnificent army for changing the problems children face in so many places.
- Ministry to children can energize every church by using every person in some way.
- Ministry to children provides Christian marriage and family models. Think of the impact on the nation if thousands of children could experience real-life examples of healthy married Christian people. One teenager from a dysfunctional home was overheard to remark, "I didn't know people could have a happy family. The

people at church have given me a goal for my life and marriage that I have never seen before."

A Testimony: How the Church Is Raising My Kids

When he heard of this book, Arnold Thomas, a member of my (Neil's) mentoring group, volunteered to tell how the church serves his family. Here's his moving first-person essay:

Ruby was the first. She worked in the nursery where we took Suzanne. They became good buddies. Even when Suzanne became a toddler and could have gone into the room with the bigger kids, she stayed with Ruby to take care of the "little babies."

When Suzanne became ill with leukemia, there were Ingrid and Denise. They took care of Suzanne sometimes. Or they would help her stressed-out parents. They occasionally went with Suzanne and her "mommy" to chemotherapy treatments. They were there when she died at age four and helped with the funeral. Bill prayed and fasted for Suzanne and us every Monday for a year before she died.

Seven-year-old Christy's buddies are Karen, the Sunday school superintendent's wife; Karen, the pastor's wife; and "Miss Judy." Dick and Norma are "adopted" Grandma and Grandpa. And there are "Cousins" Melissa, Anthony, Jeremy, and Baby Austin.

Audrey, at eleven, is our oldest. She has a boyfriend, Jim, who isn't a boyfriend; they're "just friends." Joe and Janet are doing such a great job raising Jim and his brother, Toby. My wife, Mary, and I are pleased that Audrey has the opportunity to experience such a healthy relationship at an early age. Monique is Audrey's "older sister."

This is our church family empowering our biological family. We are related by rebirth rather than by natural birth. We are not blood relatives, but by the adoptive family bond Christ provides. They are aunts, uncles, fathers, mothers, brothers, sisters, and cousins just like Jesus promised. They are examples—whether good, bad, or mediocre—for my kids to live by. They love my kids and then give them back when they've had enough.

The church is helping us raise our kids, and I am grateful. The government cannot raise my children. It is too powerful, awkward, and dangerous. My town cannot raise my children. Neighbors are transient, aloof, and wary. Our family—the church—knows us, loves us, and treats us as kin.

Here's the secret of all this. Governments, communities, churches, or cultures can only adequately impact or raise children to the extent that they assume and communicate the characteristics of a family. The family relationships of the church—just being there intimately, lovingly, and consistently—are what make kids grow.

NOTES

1. Charles M. Sell, *Family Ministry* (Grand Rapids: Zondervan, 1995), 20.

2. James Dobson and Gary L. Bauer, *Children at Risk* (Dallas: Word, 1990), 22, 23.

3. Sell, *Family Ministry,* 21.

4. Ibid., 27.

5. Ibid.

6. Wavelyn Beltz Dreher, unpublished essay, 1996. Used by permission.

7. As told to Dr. Miriam Hall and taken from an unpublished speech.

8. Dr. Miriam Hall in an unpublished speech.

9. As told to Dr. Miriam Hall and taken from an unpublished speech.

10. Ibid.

Chapter 8

FAMILY TRAITS OF CHILD-SENSITIVE CHURCHES

Boys and Girls Loved Here

Ministry to children and families is the central contemporary challenge facing the family of God. Though most congregations offer family ministries, something much deeper and more basic is needed. That is, a sense in which ministry to children and families is actually the church's main reason for existence. The authentic church incarnates family ministries. This authenticity shows in the spirit of the congregation. Such a church ministers to families by the way people relate to one another, by the way persons are cherished, and by the way the church's loving atmosphere spills over into the atmosphere of the homes.

Some church persons argue that it is a mistake to call a church a family even though that is precisely what the apostle Paul did. In our society, overusing the word *family* is becoming common. We speak of the First Church family, a swim team family, or a school faculty family. However, in the purest use of the word *family*, we mean a married couple and their biologically related relatives.

Family specialist Charles Sell makes the point that there are unique differences between families and other social groups. He outlines the distinctives:

- Family members do not choose their relationship as group members can.
- Families get children ready to leave while groups want members to stay together.
- Families are for intimacy and groups are for shared interests.
- Families are generally smaller than groups and thus function differently.[1]

Though the family of God or the community of faith is similar to other groups, it is significantly different. It is to be redemptive and relationally unique. The church is to offer meaning and belonging centered on an individual's relationship to Christ, and the church keeps healthy by loving relationships among its members. Though a church sometimes functions as a business, clique, club, or team, it was designed to function best as a family. That's why we are eager for churches everywhere to really be the family of God that cares for children.

We want children and parents to be lovingly adopted and fully accepted into the family of God because of their relationship to the Lord Christ. We pray that the church will be like a caring family to all the alienated children of the nation. We wish that each church would respond like a caring family to the cries of children everywhere.

The family church we have in mind is a loving fellowship where people know one another by name, where people meet face-to-face, where people feel they belong, where people really care for one another emotionally and spiritually, and where people meet frequently to talk about family relationships with the Father and their elder brother, Jesus Christ. We envision spiritually and emotionally healthy churches that encourage healthy Christian families and a community of faith that cares for its own children as well as children who have no biological or church family.

Above all else, the family of God must be a human-divine connection where children experience wholesome relationships. The main operational standard for the family of God is that it follow the principles of Jesus and that it empower healthy human relationships just as He did. The church must be more than what one critic complained, "The church is like a theater; the only difference is that in the theater people pay to get in, and in church they pay to get out."

Nicholas Stinnett's list of measurements for evaluating a healthy human family can be applied to evaluating a healthy church family:

1. Members express appreciation for each other.
2. Members spend time together because they enjoy being together.
3. Members have a high degree of commitment to each other.
4. Members have effective communication patterns, though they may sometimes disagree.
5. Members have concern for each other's spiritual life.
6. Members unite to deal with crises wherever they arise.[2]

What a magnetic attraction and what a high standard. To serve children, a church must be more than a crowd.

Becoming a Child-Sensitive Church

To capture the hearts of children for Christ, the church must be genuinely loving, caring, welcoming, accepting, and forgiving. The church's primary purpose must be to present Christ to all people, especially to children. That means a congregation commits in every way possible to introducing children to Jesus—the special Friend of children. To accomplish this, six family traits or characteristics must be present or put into place.

Family Trait #1: Ministry to Families Is Tied to Mission

Some may think we overstate the case to say the church must have ministry to families as its mission. Let us explain more clearly. The church's primary mission, of course, is serving Christ, but that is done most effectively through caring relationships. Serving Christ is by ministry to intact families and to broken families. The church also fulfills its mission by showing love and acceptance to those who do not have traditional family patterns, such as those who have been battered emotionally and spiritually by teenage pregnancies, abusive marriages, divorce, difficult aging parents, or parent-child conflict. It is out of its family-of-God strengths that a church helps and heals hurting people.

The primary family ministry, then, of churches that tie mission and family ministry together is a way of life rather than a strategy or program. Diana Garland explains the connection in an insightful article, "Strengthening Families and Churches in Turbulent Times":

> Family ministry is not a "new" ministry, something "extra" for the church which can afford it, the last program to be added when the worship and Bible study and music programs are in place. . . . The challenge for congregations, rather, is to adopt family ministry as a perspective from which to view the entire life and activity of the congregation, not just those programs that carry content readily identifiable as "family."[3]

In this view, caring for children and families stands at the heart of why a church exists. It is as much a mind-set of church members as it is something they do. Such a church serves children with a two-dimensional thrust, as Richard Dobbins suggests: "My hope for the family of God is firmly anchored in my conviction that the family of God must become a surrogate family for those whose families are broken and, at the same time, must remain a strong spiritual source for those whose families are intact."[4] The two dimensions strengthen and support and focus each other.

Here's how it worked for Amy:

When I was in kindergarten, I began attending Sunday school. Sometimes I took the bus; other times I walked. One way or another, I got there.

One Sunday my teacher said that Jesus loved me even when others didn't. She said He would forgive me for the wrong things I had done. Then, I understood that Jesus wasn't just in pictures or in the Bible—He was a real person. I asked Jesus to be my Savior when I was six years old.

I asked my mom to go to church with me time and time again. She made lots of excuses, but no promises. One day, however, she did go with me. That day she asked Jesus to be her Savior. It was like getting a new mom. She stopped smoking and drinking. I would hear her praying for my dad and others.

Through one Sunday school teacher reaching one student, my mother and my grandmother came to meaningful faith in Christ. Seventeen years later, my grandfather was saved. I am eternally grateful to my shy kindergarten Sunday school teacher who had the commitment to teach young children about Christ.[5]

Many churches have reason to rejoice that they are already churches where ministry to families vitally permeates their fabric. What an affirming environment for children to formulate faith. What an opportunity place for children to become personally related to human beings who model God's faithful grace. Preaching, teaching, evangelism, and worship for children and adults, too, are always more effective in warm family churches.

Family Trait #2: The Church Refuses to Be Overwhelmed by Diversity and Instability

One Christian psychologist observed that every society in the world except ours expects its children to grow up into normal adults.[6] We worry a lot about our children's future even as we allow society to stay on a collision course toward disaster.

Churches are often maligned for not doing more about all the problems children experience. These arguments say that all congregations in North America working together on family issues could stem the tide. At first, that evaluation sounds accurate and indicts churches for not doing more. The great hindrances, however, may be the church's confusion about contemporary family patterns, alternative lifestyles, and the widely accepted notion that government can solve family problems. With an intention of keeping itself pure, the church may find it easy to ignore the spiritual and emotional needs of children who are not in traditional two-parent families.

If you want to see church members shift nervously in the pews, let the pastor announce a sermon about abortion, adultery, divorce, single parenting, or homosexual issues.

Some ministers take the position that if a congregation gets uncomfortable with such subjects, it can just be uncomfortable. That may be so. But our point is that congregations that feel uncomfortable merely hearing what Scripture says about these matters will have lots of problems facing issues that children face, much less solving them. Neither will such congregations welcome having their spiritual leaders discuss diverse family structures that are popping up like poisonous weeds in our moral gardens, such as homosexual marriages or cohabitation.

Of course, the church cannot accept every kind of family diversity, nor should it do so. At the same time, the church must recognize these changes are taking place and decide whether it can serve children in new family lifestyles without compromising biblical absolutes. When children are being damaged in so many ways, often by these problem lifestyles, the church must move beyond what it cannot do to decide what it can do and then do it.

Surely, every church can minister to an infant with AIDS contracted at birth from her mother. Surely, every church can reach out to a single teenage mother whose baby is not responsible for the sins of his parents. Surely, every church can do something to care for abused women and their children. Surely, every church can love troubled children who have been taken out of abusive biological families and are being nurtured by foster families. Surely, every church can provide something like a mother's day out for women who are overstressed from spending twenty-four hours a day with their preschool-age children. Surely, every church can do something about the latchkey kids who go home to empty houses every day. Surely, every church can find a volunteer or two to work in a troubled school. Surely . . . surely . . . surely.

One of the focus study groups from a national survey group offered this observation: "The ideal family is getting hard to come by. But I do think that regardless of what's left of the family—whether it's a father and son, mother and children, or whatever—you can still have a lot of working together and playing together. And teaching the basic human values about how to treat people and how to be a good person. That's what family is all about."[7] That sounds right, but more is needed. Whatever is left of the family needs the love of Christ and the message of the gospel—the church's main business.

While suggesting ways churches can accept and help single parents and broken families, Dr. James Dobson offers this insightful and practical wisdom:

> If I understand biblical imperatives correctly, it is the task of intact families to extend a helping hand. The Lord has a special place in His heart for widows (including rejected husbands and wives) and fatherless children. The churches that best serve these wounded families usually offer these kinds of assistance: Fathers invite children of divorce to recreational activities; mothers do the same for the increasing number of children being raised by single fathers; educational programs are provided; loans and gifts are offered, especially at Christmas time or when illness strikes; houses are painted and cars repaired; meals are brought over for the working mother. Perhaps most importantly, single adults are made to feel accepted and loved by the church—part of the mainstream instead of the periphery.[8]

One congregation can't solve every family problem or heal every hurting child because the raging sea of broken families is too great. One church can't save them all, but remember the starfish story told by Jack Canfield and Mark

Hansen: A man walking along a beach saw another who was picking up something and throwing it into the water. As they came closer to each other, the first man noticed that the other was picking up starfish that had been washed up on the beach and throwing them back into the water. The man was puzzled and asked the stranger what he was doing. He replied that he was throwing the starfish back into the ocean because if they were not thrown back they would die.

"I understand," the first man replied, "but there are thousands of starfish on this beach. You can't possibly get to all of them. What difference will it make?" The other man smiled, bent down, and picked up another starfish. As he threw it back into the ocean, he remarked, "It made a difference to that one!"[9] That's what needs to happen in revolutionizing our care for children. We can make a life-changing difference to the one we save through the family of God.

However, the place of beginning to implement each of these small miracles is realizing that a particular child needs a church just like yours. God does not expect one church to do everything, but He calls every church to do what it can. Every community of faith must hear God calling them to a hurting, crying child. No congregation should feel guilty because it can't do everything, but it should be troubled if it is not doing anything to save kids.

Family Trait #3: The Family and the Church Intentionally Support Each Other

Strong families build strong churches, and strong churches build strong families. A church should make every effort to show members of a family how to be a community of faith to one another, something like the biblical idea of the church at your house. Richard Olson and Joe H. Leonard, Jr., suggest people are grateful when they find a church that

- has a vision as to what individual families can be;
- protects and provides advocacy for families;
- confronts abusive behavior and helps deliver children from such settings;
- offers training and information about family matters;
- helps families aspire to be all they can be.[10]

Their list needs the transformation of the gospel added to it. Without that revolutionary factor, most of what we do for children and families will be wasted effort.

Above all else, the church and the family must work together. No competition is allowed for time, money, or energy; in place of competition, family and church must supplement and enrich each other. Two fears are being voiced these days about the family/church partnership. Some church leaders fear that a church can become too family oriented so the priority of family always comes first before kingdom interests. Other church leaders fear that the church schedules too much for families so they have no time to know one another or to care for each other's needs. As is the case for so many issues in Christian living, a balance is needed but is difficult to achieve. Author Rodney Clapp is said to have coined a term *hyperfamilism,* which is used to describe a commitment to spend so much time enriching the family that there is no time for other interests and responsibilities.[11] Such a situation is as lopsided as devoting too much time to church activities.

I (Neil) once served a wonderful family who bought a weekend mountain cabin they used so frequently that their children became unplugged at church and lost interest.

They put family first in an out-of-balance way and defeated their primary goals. We suggest that a church plan ministry so that family members go to church at the same time even if they are involved in different activities there. An example might be midweek programming where families meet for a meal before the age grouping programs start; then the family might eat together, sing together, meet friends together, and travel to and from church together.

Another way church and family can enrich each other is to eliminate some committee and decision group meetings at the church. How many meetings do we actually need to operate a healthy church? How does all the church's committee work contribute to family wholeness? Perhaps with a little more imagination and planning we could become more efficient in the meetings we call.

Charles Sell offers this powerful insight about a healthy connection between home and church:

> God has given us all things to enjoy, including marriage and family. Certainly we should not allow our enjoyment of marriage to interfere with our commitment to church, for example having too frequent romantic weekends that exclude Sunday church involvement. But neither should we permit enjoyment of church to the neglect of our family life, as when church members immerse themselves in church work at the expense of their spouses and children. There may be times when we temporarily sacrifice family for church (during crises or special missions) or church for family (as when one's mate's illness demands a special person's time). But while temporary sacrifice is proper, abandonment is not. . . . Seeing both the temporary and eternal qualities of marriage and family will keep us from unduly idolizing them while at the same time not underrating their importance.[12]

In this enrichment process, a church should sometimes plan activities that involve people across generations. A church can offer ways for family members to strengthen their relationships at home, such as marriage enrichment and parenting classes and parent-child meetings with Sunday school staffers. Meetings at church should be planned to make us better Christians and to make stronger churches and to build better families. To make this happen, we must continually evaluate the family and the church.

The goal in all this is to be sure home and church each contributes to the strength of the other. Building a church-at-your-home concept for ourselves shines through this paragraph written by Pastor Paul Caminiti:

> The verbs in Moses' provocation speech to Israel's families remind me that it takes large chunks of time to grow a family. Parents were commanded to teach and talk to their children "when you *sit* in your house and when you *walk* by the way and when you *lie down* and when you *rise up*" (Deut. 6:7). I like to think of these as "home-grown" verbs. They convince me God is unhappy with rampant absenteeism that prevails in too many of our homes.[13]

The question of how the church and the home can enrich each other is summarized in an interview with Dr. James Dobson in *Leadership* magazine. When asked, "What has been the most effective family ministry you've seen in churches?" Dobson replied,

> Perhaps I sound old fashioned, but the greatest contribution the church can make is to draw families to the person of Jesus Christ in an attitude of genuine repentance and renewal. Nothing brings husbands, wives, and children together more effectively than a face-to-face encounter with the Cre-

ator of families. In fact, it is almost impossible to stand in His holy presence without recognizing our own pettiness and resentment and selfishness with those closest to us. When I was a child, we used to sing a folk-gospel song entitled "The Old-Time Religion." One verse stated, "It makes you love everybody." That's still true.[14]

Perhaps our word *enrichment* is not strong enough when we consider Dobson's statement from that same interview: "The church is the first line of defense of the family. . . . We need fellowship with believers, we need reinforcement from those of like mind, and we need biblical exegesis from someone trained to explain the Word. We need the church."[15] Certainly, the home and the church need each other—it is an absolute necessity that the home and the church work together to save the children of our own homes and to save children who have no Christian homes.

So we see that God planned for the family and the church to work together to nurture children spiritually. Problems arise when one partner fails to carry out its responsibilities or attempts to usurp the role of the other partner. Unfortunately, as Robert J. Choun, Jr., and Michael S. Lawson point out, many families fail to carry out their biblical mandate to provide spiritual nurture for children. As they note, that puts even more responsibility on the church:

> In reality, the church may need to carry the bulk of the responsibility. Protestant educators have hesitated to say this clearly. The modern collapse of the family puts the church squarely in the position of needing to strengthen both the family unit and the individuals within it.
>
> The home was once the center of Christian nurture. Now child abuse, working mothers, and single-parent families lead

a long list of stresses that presently sap the strength of this fundamental Christian education agency. By the time repairs occur in the home, the nurturing years for children have too often slipped silently away. Without question, the Bible makes the home responsible for Christian education. Yet in their present condition, families may be unable to fulfill the call to Christian education. If the home fails, either the church fills the void or the task remains undone.[16]

Let's admit it's a tough task for the church to take the heaviest end of this crushing load. But for many children, it will not be carried out if the church doesn't do it.

Family Trait #4: The Church Maintains a Child-Sensitive Environment

The pressing question here is, Are children welcome at your church? A child-sensitive environment is as much spirit and attitude as it is facilities, equipment, and personnel. A child-sensitive church has a climate where all kinds of families feel comfortable—traditional families, blended families, single-parent families, children without families, foster families, no-children couples, singles, and bicultural families.

Child-sensitive churches give children priority and visibility so kids sing in the public services, kids help with ushering, and kids sometimes read Scripture aloud in public adult services. In these churches, the ministry to children is highly visible, and facilities are well marked. Nursery facilities are close to the entrance. Grandparent types reach out to children in the hallways.

These churches view children as the church of today as well as the church of tomorrow. They work hard to know children's names and to provide a safe haven for children who live their whole lives in brokenness.

Many of these churches provide network families of persons or groups who are responsible for making children and their families welcome. That may mean finding a substitute grandparent contact. That may mean putting a newly divorced parent in touch with a parent who worked through a divorce with the help of the church. Or that may mean putting a couple with their first baby in touch with a couple who have a year-old first child.

Child-sensitive churches are aware that children from blended families will not be able to attend church functions as often as those who live in unbroken families. Blended children are often forced to miss church activities because they spend alternate weekends with the parent with whom they do not live. Sometimes children can work through these conflicts of calendars if church activities are scheduled far enough in advance. However, special care must be taken to avoid any public mention in Sunday school classes or youth groups that "Sally can't come since she has to spend that weekend with her father because her parents are divorced."

A few years ago, I (Neil) attended one of the historic churches in New York City for a worship service. The bulletin announced that a child would be dedicated to the Lord during that service. Let's call the child Jonathan Earl Smith. The pastor asked, "Will Jonathan bring his parents and grandparents forward for the dedication?" The pastor also asked the parents to bring their other children forward, even as he invited a Sunday school teacher who worked with toddlers in the church nursery to come forward. With these simple but thoughtful touches, the pastor tied the church and the family together. The unspoken words said, "Children are important here."

Family Trait #5: The Church Is an Advocate for Children

Focus on the Family has served children well as it has urged Christian people to become advocates for children at various levels of civic and national life. Since the church has a significant responsibility to children, it should see to it that communities are children friendly. Though this task may be a new role for your congregation, you will be surprised at how much influence you can have.

Advocacy for children can mean many activities or few. Whatever the level of intensity, the goal is to improve the lot of children in your community and in the nation. Advocacy may mean organizing a program for cable TV to make people aware of the needs of children. It may mean serving on committees of the PTA or school board. It may mean organizing a forum of community leaders to make your community more aware of the needs of children. In our city, one mother started a march to stop gang violence. Much to her surprise, other parents and teens joined her. Soon she was being interviewed on local TV news programs, organizing community forums, and networking with a high school principal to add preventive measures on the high school campus.

Advocacy may mean writing or calling on a government official to ask how you can help. At other times, advocacy may mean offering the church's facilities for the use of community groups, such as AA, Mothers Against Drunk Drivers (MADD), or Scouts, or support information groups for parents of children with disabilities or disease.

Sometimes, advocacy is offering a program to inform people about what is happening to harm children in our communities. At other times, it is taking the part of a child who needs someone to speak up for him in school or in the community. Or it is about dealing with a harmful bureaucratic practice of a social service agency—for example, in foster care or adoptions.

Advocacy essentially means the church actively asks every part of society to make it possible for children to feel safe and sound and cherished. Advocacy efforts for children need not be grand or big. You will be surprised how responsive government leaders will be to your concerns if you express them kindly, insistently, and frequently. Every member of your church can do something so that children are treated better and safer and kinder.

Advocacy might even use the Quaker idea of providing clearness meetings. A clearness meeting offers individuals or families a group of six to ten people with whom they can discuss an impending decision or opportunity for service. In a clearness meeting, the group asks questions of those who face a decision, and the group, in turn, provides insights and perspectives. At the close of the meeting, the group prays for those who are to make the decision. Then the decision is left to the individuals, but they feel supported by the group.

Think what such a meeting could mean for persons in moral confusion or in a quandary about divorce. Think, too, about how the concept might be used in community service agencies facing difficult ethical decisions that shape the policies such groups later impose on children and their families.

Family Trait #6: The Church Becomes an Extended Family for Children

Elsewhere in this book, we have discussed how and why a church can be an extended family to children. Increasing numbers of children do not live near their extended families, but they still need uncles and aunts, cousins and grandparents to affirm, hug, encourage, teach, love, cheer, and sometimes spoil. They need an extended family in times of joy as well as times of sadness. Children miss having their grandparents at church, ball games, and birthday parties. Children, though they don't know it and cannot explain it, miss having an extended family to help their mom and dad be better parents. Since creation, extended families have helped parents raise their sons and daughters; living nearby made it easy for young parents to seek and follow the guidance of the older generation or generations.

Every church, with a little intentionality, can become more like an extended family in a child's life. In every church's ministry, structure, and mode of operation, it can intentionally implement ways to become a family to families. It can welcome into its heart children, teens, unmarried persons, orphans, blended families, newlyweds, and persons from every generation.

We love the tender idea Jack and Judith Balswick used to close their book, *The Family*: "When Jesus therefore saw His mother, and the disciple whom He loved standing by, He said to His mother, 'Woman, behold your son!' Then He said to the disciple, 'Behold your mother!' And from that hour that disciple took her to his own home" (John 19:26–27). Then the Balswicks suggest, "Our goal in relationships should be to so forgive, empower, and intimately know one another so that Jesus would want to send His mother to be a part of our family."[17]

For the purposes of developing an adopted extended family in the church, let's rephrase the Balswicks' sentence: Our goal for relationships in the church should be to so forgive, love, and intimately care for children so that Jesus would want every child to be a part of the family of God that meets at your church.

"Aren't They All Our Children?"

Senator Sam Nunn told a story that happened in Bosnia. A little girl was hit by a sniper in the tragic conflict in the middle of Sarajevo.

At the moment of the shocking pain, a reporter dropped his pencil and pad and rushed to the man who was holding the child and helped them both into his car.

As the reporter stepped on the accelerator, racing to the hospital, the man holding the bleeding child said, "Hurry, my friend, my child is still alive." A moment or two later, "Hurry, my friend, my child is still breathing." A moment later, "Hurry, my friend, my child is still warm." Finally, "Hurry. Oh my God, my child is getting cold."

When they got to the hospital, the little girl had died. As the two men were . . . washing the blood off their hands and clothes, the man turned to the reporter and said, "This is a terrible task for me. I must go tell her father that his child is dead. He will be heartbroken." The reporter was amazed. He looked at the grieving man and said, "I thought she was your child."

The man looked back and said, "No, but aren't they all our children?"

Senator Nunn reminded his hearers and us, "Yes, they are all our children. They are also God's children as well, and He has entrusted us with their care in Sarajevo, in Somalia, in New York City, in Los Angeles, in my hometown of Perry, Georgia, and here in Washington, D.C."[18]
Your town must be added to the list. And your church belongs on the list, too.

NOTES

1. Charles M. Sell, *Family Ministry* (Grand Rapids: Zondervan, 1995), 173–84.

2. Ibid., 161.

3. Diana Garland, "Strengthening Families and Churches in Turbulent Times," *Journal of Family Ministry* 9, 1 (1995): 5–21.

4. Richard D. Dobbins, *The Family-Friendly Church* (Altamonte Springs, Fla.: Creation House, 1989), 12.

5. As told to Dr. Miriam Hall and taken from an unpublished speech.

6. Jack O. Balswick and Judith K. Balswick, *The Family* (Grand Rapids: Baker, 1991), 109.

7. As quoted in Lee Salk, *Familyhood* (New York: Simon & Schuster, 1992), 19.

8. An interview with James Dobson, "Keys to a Family-Friendly Church," *Leadership,* winter 1986, 16.

9. Jack Canfield and Mark Victor Hansen, *Chicken Soup for the Soul* (Deerfield Beach, Fla.: Health Communications, 1993), 22.

10. Richard P. Olson and Joe H. Leonard, Jr., *A New Day for Family Ministry* (New York: Alban Institute, 1996), 82.

11. Sell, *Family Ministry,* 71.

12. Ibid., 74.

13. Paul Caminiti, "How Many Meetings Do We Need?" *Leadership,* winter, 1986, 123.

14. Dobson, "Keys to a Family Friendly Church," 13.

15. Ibid., 14.

16. Michael S. Lawson and Robert J. Choun, Jr., *Directing Christian Education* (Chicago: Moody Press, 1992), 24.

17. Balswick and Balswick, *The Family,* 306.

18. Sam Nunn, "Intellectual Honesty, Moral and Ethical Behavior," an address delivered to the National Prayer Breakfast, Washington, D.C., February 1, 1996, as printed in *Vital Speeches of the Day,* March 15, 1996, 328.

Chapter 9

CHRIST-CENTERED MARRIAGES HELP KIDS GROW

Making Home a Training Camp for Children

You've heard the advice: The best thing a parent can do for a kid is to love the other parent. The idea should be edited for our purpose: The best thing a Christian couple can do for their children is to strengthen their marriage in every way possible. A good marriage helps every kid who experiences it grow. The goal is to make every Christian marriage a training camp for the natural children from that marriage and to provide a model for every child who observes from outside the family.

"Why talk about marriage and family?" a family specialist asked. Then he quickly answered his question, "Because our own family experience is the most significant experience of our lives. As a human interaction, it has greater impact on our lives than any other experience." His view squares with our experience, doesn't it?

If the cornerstone of this book—it takes a church to raise strong, healthy kids—is right, then the church must do everything it can to build strong marriages and grow healthy homes. Since a desire for a strong Christ-centered marriage is more often caught than taught, the church must work to be a laboratory of healthy family relationships. Many kids will never see anything faintly resembling a strong marriage unless they see it in families at church.

While marriage building may not be a church's only priority, we must consider one marriage ministry specialist's assessment: "The heart of family ministry is the nature of the church, not merely its work."[1] Serving people and helping them develop healthy Christian relationships at home are at the heart of the church's work. For that reason, discussion of ministry to children must include a discussion of how to make marriages work better.

Marriage Conflict Is Real

Have you heard about the pastor, fresh from seminary, who meant well but made his congregation laugh out loud when he said, "Genuine Christian families will never have problems getting along with each other"? Since he was new in the ministry and had never been married, he had lots to learn about how Christian marriages work. His congregation overlooked his mistake because of his inexperience. But that pastor represents a commonplace naivete about marriage, family, and child rearing.

We sometimes have gigantic problems in our most primary relationships simply because we are human. Though we are believers, we may be grossly inexperienced in how we interact with the most important people in our lives. We are green with immaturity in handling problems in our marriages even as we are inexperienced in applying faith to our parenting. Conflicts sometimes occur in even the best marriages. The secret of a good marriage, however, is to learn to apply faith to the details of our relationships and continually ask ourselves how Christ wants our homes to be. That's what the church must help us do.

The church has to resource and strengthen families. As this effort enhances health and wholeness for marriage partners, it will also influence the next generation and beyond. The measure in which marriages of persons in the church succeed affects all children, even as it helps them learn how to establish their own homes. Stronger marriages make stronger churches and stronger children.

Marriage Is Here to Stay

The fastest growing marital status category is "divorced." The number of currently divorced adults quadrupled from 4.3 million in 1970 to 17.4 million in 1994.[2] The dramatic rise in divorces has shaken young adults' confidence in marriage and has damaged lots of kids. Many young people we talk with express a skepticism about marriage because they don't think people can get along well enough to commit to a lifelong relationship. In fact, adults who have never married have become one of the fastest growing segments of the adult population.[3] The rise in divorces and the delay in first marriages among adults are two major factors contributing to the growing proportion of children in one-parent living situations.[4] Might it be because so many believe it is either impossible or extremely difficult to have a strong marriage? These impressions, or perhaps they are evaluations, come from observing the marriages of their parents and friends. Some young adults say they want a relationship like their friend's parents' marriage but not one like their own parents' relationship.

But we know marriage is here to stay. From 75 percent to 80 percent of all marriages are solemnized by the church or organized religion; this means America's pastors, priests, and rabbis continue to have at least some access to most couples. If these leaders commit to marriage counseling and speak of its value, the institution of marriage will be significantly strengthened.[5] As we talk to people we meet along the way, we find that nearly all of them would marry the same person again, and even those who have been divorced plan on getting married again. In one Barna survey, when asked the question, "Did God intend for people to get married and stay in that relationship for life?" 80 percent of married persons answered yes, and 76 percent of divorced persons said yes.[6] In other words, the institution of marriage is here to stay. We just need to figure out how to make marriages stronger so they thrive for a lifetime.

Ties That Hold Marriages Together

Let's consider five fundamental ties for couples to reinforce in their marriages and for the church to teach to strengthen marriages. For the emotional and spiritual development of boys and girls, parents in the church should widely practice and share these ideas. Children need to learn about these ties so they can begin forming ideas about their own marriages early on. Without powerful shaping influences from the church, our young people are likely to repeat the same mistakes their parents made, and the generational downward spiral will not be stopped.

Family Tie #1: Be Willing to Give

The prospects of having a healthy marriage are not very high unless both partners give themselves wholly to the relationship. Every marriage demands self-giving love. Each partner has to give a lot, or any marriage flounders.

When partners really love each other, each must be willing to accept the other. Though both partners change throughout the years of any marriage, one should never be the other partner's remodeling project. I (H. B.) love the threefold possibilities in Dr. Richard Kremler's words, "Important factors leading to fragmentation of the home are a result of loss of understanding, giving up too soon, and unreasonable expectations."[7] Let's make the idea more positive by turning his comment around. We can have strong, effective, and satisfying marriages by cultivating understanding, by persevering, and by keeping our expectations realistic.

In building a strong marriage and a happy family, try asking yourself these questions before you ask them of anybody else: (1) Are my expectations realistic? (2) Is there something happening in my mate's life that explains his or her actions? (3) Am I willing to listen creatively when my spouse has problems?

Issues outside the home may complicate a spouse's life more than we can imagine. That's when a spouse needs understanding. Being aware of these possibilities helps. Someone said of her long-term marriage, "We have built a terrific relationship, not because we were instantly compatible, but because we were intensely committed."[8]

Most of these same questions can be applied to parenting relationships and awareness. Consider what takes place when Johnny wants to play basketball more than anything else in the world. He goes out for the team, makes the first and second cut, and then finds there are not enough uniforms to go around. He is not chosen for the team. He comes home glum, goes to his room, slams the door, and thinks life is over.

The unthinking father goes to Johnny's room and says, "Johnny, we don't act that way around here. Straighten up. Basketball's not the biggest thing in the world, and you should know that." But to Johnny, basketball is the most important thing in his world. That is why Johnny is heartbroken, but he is also hurt because no one seems to understand.

How much better for the father to go upstairs, knock on the door, and ask Johnny if he can come in. Then the father sits on the bed and is quiet for a moment. Then he says, "Johnny, I probably never told you before, but I was cut from the team once. I don't know all you are feeling, but I know a little bit about how it hurts. Johnny, why don't we start playing hoops together? Then you can try again next year. I want you to know, son, how proud I am of you. Now let's go eat supper. Your mother and I would love to be with you. It might help you get your mind on other things. We love you, son."

The whole idea is trying to understand how another family member is feeling. It works in parenting as well as in marriage. Many children never see parents putting themselves out for kids.

Caring deeply for another means we give other family members the right to express their opinions and space to develop their uniqueness. This right does not mean parents give up setting standards for family behavior, but it teaches children how to state their opinions, how to consider consequences, and how to be loving even to people who disagree with them.

Somewhere we heard about a woman in marriage counseling who said of her husband, "Oh, I believe he has a right to his own opinion; I just don't want to hear it." That's a common problem in many marriages. In a world of conflict, we need to give family members a right to speak their own opinions. We need to give them the right to discuss and even disagree with our ideas. In this process children learn about love and acceptance and belonging. And children from dysfunctional homes whom we adopt at church will also be affected by this policy of freedom to speak when they see it in action in our families.

Family Tie #2: Speak the Truth in Love and Ask Big Questions

Ephesians 4:15 says we are to speak the truth in love. Among other things, that means we will speak up when we see others about to destroy themselves by improper behavior, negative habits, or harmful attitudes. Too long some Christians have believed that keeping quiet—minding their own business, it is called—was the only way Christians could keep their speech holy and influential. But there is much more to this speaking and being quiet. We must seek to help people we love in the family and in the community of faith avoid the consequences of harmful actions and self-induced difficulties.

How is that done? Speak the truth in love. Make every effort to assess the reason for the problem and come to a helpful solution.

One effective Christian counselor told me (H. B.) that

"every marriage or family problem I see is a result of people asking no questions or asking small questions." Think of the implications of that statement. What are the big questions? Here are several for openers: (1) Why is this happening? (2) Why are we feeling pain? (3) Why are we irritable and moody? and (4) Why am I silent?

The second set of questions is personal and more inner-directed. These questions help us keep from blaming others for our problems and help us understand our part in difficulties: (1) How has my behavior or attitude contributed to this misunderstanding? (2) Have I been selfish? (3) Am I insensitive? (4) How have I been irresponsible? and (5) Have I been stubborn?

The third set of big questions has to do with applying faith to the details of a marriage or in relationships to children. These questions bring the Bible and our relationship to Christ into the conflict—and that can be either soothing or convicting: (1) Are my faith and my handling of this situation consistent? (2) Am I practicing my faith in this situation? (3) What would Jesus do in this relationship? (4) Are my behavior and attitude pleasing to God? (5) Could I live with my spouse and children acting the way I am in our future relationships? and (6) What am I doing in this conflict that would make the people I most love become more like Christ?

To have Christ-exalting marriages and families, we must be willing to ask the big questions—to speak the truth in love and to use the truth we discover to change our conduct into living that honors Christ.

After months of senseless teen rebellion, Kevin was influenced by a youth pastor who practiced tough love—one who was willing to listen and to hold the boy accountable. The youth pastor refused to allow Kevin to get by with actions or attitudes that were detrimental to his emotional, physical, or spiritual well-being. In trying to explain the relationship, Kevin told his mother, "Mom, this guy really loves me." Kevin's mother, threatened by this new person in her son's life, said, "I love you, too, son. You know that. I love you very much." Kevin replied, "Yes, Mom, I know. But he tries to understand the way I think. He accepts me in spite of my faults. And he doesn't take any excuses from me."

Love is necessary, but it is not enough. To have strong marriages and healthy families, we must be bold and brave enough to ask the big questions so we can understand the other's behavior, so we can put ourselves in another's position, so we can understand our own behavior, and so we can personally change at the precise points where change is most needed.

Asking and answering these tough questions help us get to the main point of what troubles our relationships and help us keep from irrationally blaming others for difficulties we create for ourselves.

Think about how important this process is for the children of our homes and the children of our churches. Though the concept may not be easy for them to grasp, its demonstration will affect them in ways beyond anything we can imagine.

Family Tie #3: Practice the Golden Rule and Follow the Winners

Let's think seriously about reestablishing the golden rule in our families. It could make such a redemptive difference. What if parents tried to become kids again so they could see how tough it is to face the temptations that pull many kids down at school these days? What would happen if parents could really understand the peer pressure, the drugs, the pregnancies, the doubt, the fear, the abuse, the guns, and the gangs?

One of the pressing, seldom-discussed tough human development spots is that every stage takes a person through many new experiences. Think what that means to the girl who goes to school for the first time, to the boy who finds the first hair on his chest or hears his voice start to change, to newlyweds who come home from their wedding trip to decide who will keep the checkbook, or to the older person who spends his first night in a rest home. There are a thousand places along the human journey where we need folks to apply the golden rule to their relationships with us. And there are just as many places where we need to apply the golden rule to our relationships with them!

If everyone in the family practiced the golden rule, we would begin to realize how things feel and look to each other. Then we could be more accepting and loving at home—making home and family a sanctuary where we experience peace and acceptance and strength.

I (H. B.) like to think of 1 Corinthians 13:4–7 as the credo for Christian marriage and family life: "Love . . . is kind . . . thinks no evil; does not rejoice in iniquity, but rejoices in the truth; bears all things, believes all things, hopes all things, endures all things." That's so much different from the all-too-common idea that "home is where you are treated the best but grumble the most."

No one can build a satisfying home alone. Every family member has to be brought into the process and start to see home as a special place for spiritual refueling and emotional renewal. I (H. B.) enjoy telling people that if they want happy homes, they must follow winners. That is, look for those who succeed in family relationships, and try to duplicate what they are doing and saying and thinking. Learn from the champions, and replicate what works in their primary relationships. The winning families seek first the kingdom of God. Strength and empowerment flow from a settled set of the will to put God first in everything that relates to the family. This kingdom-first lifestyle is the most satisfying life to be found anywhere.

I (H. B.) remember a family that had a strong influence on our family. In many ways they taught our boys strong, accepting behavior that shows even now in the families our sons have established. Their style of life was contagious. When they were together, we could tell they were proud of one another, and they respected their father and were deeply proud of their mother. They were attentive and polite to one another. When difficulties came, they moved in to support and love and lift. Supportive behavior seemed natural to them. They never raised their voices. As Scripture teaches, they refused to provoke one another to anger, but they kept encouraging one another to be the best that they could be. Follow the example of people like that.

Strong marriages practice the golden rule and imitate winners.

Family Tie #4: Practice Forgiveness and Build Each Other Up

In Ephesians 4:32, Paul wrote to the church at Ephesus that they were to "be kind to one another, tenderhearted, forgiving one another, even as God in Christ forgave you." What an order, and what a gift to another, and what a relief to us. Forgiveness is to relationships what oil is to a machine—we cannot operate without it. Jesus and Paul and all serious Christian disciples through the centuries have realized that forgiveness is an absolute necessity. And it still is.

One of the greatest deterrents to satisfying family living is living with unforgiveness toward another family member. We owe it to each other and to ourselves to set a mood in our homes that is open and free and relaxed and forgiving. The apostle Paul offered good spiritual direction and sound emotional counsel when he said, "Do not let the sun go down on your wrath" (Eph. 4:26). Closing a day without repairing a misunderstanding means we will have a troubling night, and tomorrow will be more of what we had today. Lack of forgiveness in family relationships has a way of accumulating over time so the home becomes filled with tension and sensitivities and misery—all unnecessary when forgiveness is so available to all of us.

To live in human relationships is to experience and to cause injustices, wrongs, mistakes, and inconsistencies. Just the opposite is needed. An unforgiving spirit and a failure to try to forget caused great grief in many families. It is possible to hold on to grudges to the point that we make ourselves miserable and our future ghastly. Healthy families know how to forgive and forget.

One way to cultivate forgiveness is for each of us to ask concerning our family relationships, What kind of friend am I? I (H. B.) often raise that question in family counseling. People often respond by saying, "What do you mean, what kind of friends are we? We're married. We're brothers and sisters. We live in the same house. What do you mean, what kind of friends are we?"

I hasten to add, "How do friends treat each other?" Then I remind them, "Friends say, 'I'm sorry,' when they offend each other. Friends give compliments to each other when one does something admirable. They say, 'That's okay,' when others have done them wrong. Friends, rather than hold a grudge or get angry, value each other. They encourage each other. They challenge each other to be their very best."

If families are going to be as good as they can be, family members must become authentic friends. When spouses disagree, they should ask themselves, "Why are we doing this to each other when we are so important to each other?" Or they should say to each other, "We are the most important people in the world to each other. We should be loving and building each other up." Let's be as nice and gentle to our spouse and kids as we are to our friends.

Family Tie #5: Grow Spiritually and Expect God to Build Your Home

At a trying moment in national life, Joshua announced these strong words of determined resolve: "If it seems evil to you to serve the LORD, choose for yourselves this day whom you will serve. . . . But as for me and my house, we will serve the LORD" (Josh. 24:15).

Families, churches, and the nation need thousands to make a Joshua-type commitment concerning "me and my house." Regardless of what the Smiths and the Joneses and the Greens do, you and your family have already determined your course of action. You can read all the books you want on marriage, family, and mentoring of children, but they will do little good without a commitment to make Christ head of the family.

Making Him head involves a set of the will, so He is first in all things. We make Him head of the family. We allow

Him to evaluate every conversation and decision and priority. He is the invited One—He never forces Himself into our human relationships. He is our pattern, our guide, our ideal.

In putting such a commitment in place, we already know what we will do when inevitable conflicts develop and storms come. The Lord Jesus Christ is the finest source for sound, healthy family relationships. We need to make our commitment to Him so definite that the whole family already knows how to respond when trouble comes. The deciding was done in less stressful times.

We need to think through our responses to the values of secular society before they trap us. In Romans 12:2, the apostle Paul wrote, "Do not be conformed to this world." The forces of the world will determine our values and establish our standard of morality unless we intentionally resist. The value system around us is self-centered and materialistic; that will be our value system, too, unless we resist it. Christian values need to be built into family life the same way we build in good health practices and sound nutritional habits. We must develop a fixed will that puts God first in all things.

Following God's will is never automatic. It must be intentional. But to be intentional, we must start with the idea that God always has our best interests in mind. A sad reality in our world is the failure of many Christians to follow God's will in their family. They miss God's plans for them and experience unrest, unhappiness, failure, and fragmented relationships. Years later they experience the awful harvest of family brokenness, pain, divorce, and alienation.

Why not avoid all this by instituting a Joshua-type family

commitment: "As for me and my house, we will serve the Lord"? The Joshua mind-set creates a home where God is supreme. Where God indwells our hearts to such a degree that He takes up residence. Then He directs our lives better than we could ever do on our own. He takes charge because we ask Him to do so. He leads the family in better ways than we could devise on our own. When we commit ourselves and our families as Joshua did, He leads us to incredibly fulfilling accomplishments and takes us places we never dreamed of going. His ways are ways of peace, joy, satisfaction, and accomplishment.

Once while being entertained as the honored dinner guest with a family, I (H. B.) noticed they had a chair and table setting for one more person than had arrived. The hostess called for us to come to the table. When everyone gathered, I asked if another guest was coming and suggested we might wait. The host and hostess responded, "He's already here." I was puzzled and asked them to explain. They answered, "We always set an extra plate for the Master. We have a tendency to not be as careful as we should in our speech, so the extra place setting reminds us Jesus is the listener to every conversation. We want to be sure we are as much like Him as possible. We want Jesus to know He is welcome. We want Him to dominate our lifestyle and our conversation and our values. Making a place for Him makes all the difference for us. Though some may think it strange, it is just a little thing we do to remind ourselves that we belong to Him. You might call it a holy Show-and-Tell."

Though you might not actually set a place at the table for Jesus, you can live a life of continual dependence on Him and one that welcomes Him into every action and attitude of your family.

Let's make Christ head of our families. So many forces are undermining the Christian family that we need to be more vigilant than ever. At a time when the family and the church are under attack, let's deepen our commitment and set our wills and strengthen our families. It's time for every believer to establish a Joshua mind-set in the home. We must move from a "me-driven" style of life to a Christ-driven way of living.

Will Your Family Survive?

If the Christian family in America survives, it will be because we pay whatever price it takes. We believe God will see to it that the Christian family survives in an ultimate sense, but the more pressing question for you is, Will your family survive? Will it be authentically Christian? Will it be a source of grace and love and forgiveness? Will it be fun for you and yours? And will it be a winner family that children from broken homes can take as a model for their own future families? The Lord Jesus wants you to have such a spiritually strong family, and so do you.

NOTES

1. Charles M. Sell, *Family Ministry* (Grand Rapids: Zondervan, 1995), 157.

2. Arlene F. Saluter, *Marital Status and Living Arrangements,* U.S. Bureau of the Census, March 1996, series P20-484, vi.

3. Ibid., vii.

4. Ibid., viii, ix.

5. Michael I. McManus, *National and International Religion Report,* November 1, 1993.

6. "Family in America" survey conducted February 1992 by the Barna Research Group, Ltd.

7. Charles E. Blair, *The Silent Thousands Speak,* (Grand Rapids: Zondervan, 1968), 54.

8. Ibid., 82.

PART 3
ARCHITECTS OF THE ENDURING

Chapter 10

IT'S HARD TO FORGET A CHURCH

"I Can't Get You Out of My Mind"

I have tried, but I can't forget you. My mind keeps going back to our years together." Though the sentences sound like they are from a long-forgotten flame, they come from a love letter of a much different sort. A forty-one-year-old scientist writes to a pastor of a small country church. The writer, involved in a full-blown midlife crisis, tells how he has sought fulfillment on the dead-end streets named position, prestige, and power. Now the scientist has come full circle back to contact people who nourished his faith in his childhood. His letter inquires about old Sunday school teachers and childhood church chums.

Listen as Pastor Jim reads a section from the letter to a mutual acquaintance:

I've gained professional success—more than I could have imagined—but I feel an unexplained emptiness at the center of myself I can't ignore. I want to revisit my spiritual roots to try to rebuild my faith. I am on a journey back to God, and my childhood memories from church are giving me many needed signposts. I can't get away from what the church meant to me then.

The scientist's letter sounds like the adage, "You can take the boy out of the country, but you can't take the country out of the boy." Novels, movies, TV sitcoms, and talk shows do their best to keep childhood traumas churning in our minds so that it has become almost a cultural addiction to discuss dysfunctional problems from childhood on afternoon TV. Many people enjoy blaming their parents for ruining their lives.

But isn't there another side? What about the positive Christian influences that came to us through a church? What about all those times when a Sunday school teacher showed us love, when a Scout leader answered our tough questions about God, and when other caring folks supported us through a crisis? Maybe it's time to downplay our scars and take an encouraging inventory of the nourishing experiences we have known.

To rivet truth in His hearers' minds, Jesus told unforgettable stories now called parables. That's what He did one time when the Pharisees groused about His "terrible" offense of eating with tax collectors and "sinners." Instead of defending Himself, Jesus told three stories, which can be found in Luke 15. You probably remember them. One story was about a lost sheep, another about a lost coin, and the third about a lost son.

Jesus Tells About Homecomings

The story about the son highlights the father's relationship with his two boys. It highlights warmth of home, strength of family affection, and shared inheritances; it also shows what children remember for life. Nowhere in all of literature can one find a more heartwarming example of what God means for the church to be than at the prodigal's homecoming. Love permeates the story. Unconditional acceptance without reservation is the order of the day. Celebration of renewed relationships crackles from every detail of the passage.

Think again about the younger brother, often called the prodigal. He had a consuming passion to experience the outside world. He craved firsthand experience of a more worldly lifestyle. He wanted freedom to live his own way. He even expected his father to finance his folly. And with no record of even a mild protest, that's what the father did. Every father and son can identify in some measure with the parable. It is the age-old struggle of when to go and when to stay. However, Jesus does not forget to tell about the stay-at-home, self-righteous boy who obviously represented the Pharisees to whom our Lord was speaking. A convincing argument can be made for comparing the stay-at-home son with compliant contemporary church members.

Several Bible commentators suggest everyone is represented in the story, either as the go-away son or as the stay-at-home son. The father represents God, who loves all of us with an everlasting love despite our sins or the consequences of our bad choices. However, to consider the church's task of shaping children into Christlikeness, let's look at the story through a rather unusual lens. Try to see the parable as a description of an unforgettable memory of God's gracious care for you.

Though the wandering boy traveled miles from home, he never could shake the father from his memory. As he started toward the alluring city, his newly accepted value system played tricks on him so even early in his waywardness he was forced to compare home with what he thought he would enjoy in the new setting. A rude awakening soon came, however. Even at the zenith of his far-country merriment, he felt a strong twinge of homesickness. Then when he "came to his senses" while feeding pigs, he remembered how well hired hands at his father's table ate even as he was "starving to death." Then he reasoned, "I've made a stupid mistake." So he started home, practicing his repentance speech as he walked: "I have sinned against heaven and against you. I am no longer worthy to be called your son. Make me like one of your hired men."

How Real Love Works

Regret and forgiveness, dread and welcome, selfishness and generosity, and realism and tenderness saturate the story. Much to the prodigal's surprise, the father treated him as if he had never been away. Even when the older son demonstrated ugly rage, the father showed *agape* affection.

What unmerited favor the father showed both boys. To the go-away son, the father said, "My son was lost and is found. He was dead and is alive." After reading that passage, a country preacher remarked, "That's real good news."

To the stay-at-home son, the father said, "Everything I have is yours." Of those words, the preacher said, "That's about as good as you can get."

The way the father in the story dealt with his children is a lot like the way God deals with us.

Children Can't Forget Memories

There's an important message in this story for the family of God. As a church stimulates faith development in children, the family of God must remember that children never get completely away from the Father's influence. If children wander away or choose to leave the warmth of the family home, they can never free themselves from memories of the Father and the family. Having tasted God's nearness and having received love from the church, sons and daughters can't get away from that either.

Such memories are like a brand on the soul. Everything the church invests in a child continues to be played over and over for years in the adult's mind: "How can I ever forget that a group of believers once loved me? Once someone thought I was important. Once someone told me I could come back to the Father's house 'safe and sound,' to use the parable's language."

The parable and its meaning are good news to all who take their spiritual responsibility to children seriously. Wherever the child goes, you go. Whatever the child does, you are there. Whoever the child associates with, you are there. Regardless of the intensity and depth of misery, even to feeding pigs or experiencing physical hunger, you are there, pointing the child home to God. Even down to old age, the influence of the church goes with the far-country folks as well as with the stay-at-home folks. The power of biblical memory and the impact of strong Christian influence remain forever. Memory follows the wanderer down every rebellious mile and stalks them down every spiritual detour.

Gospel Seed Takes Root

That may be what the Bible means when it advises us to train up a child in the way he should go. One rebellious forty-year-old woman said, "I just couldn't get away from the love of the church though I lived two thousand miles away in geography and twenty-five years away from my childhood." The church's influence is astonishing. Count on it. The kindness a church shows children and the stories of the faith children hear are part of the promise, "My word will not return void." The gospel seeds lodge in lots of surprising places.

Of course, many who reject God's reign in their lives like to recount bad church experiences. Admittedly, there are too many heartbreaking examples of mistreatment, but such mistreatment is not genuine Christianity. Whether we are discussing dollars, diamonds, or churches, rejecting the authentic because of once being burned by the counterfeit is self-defeating and shortsighted.

Let's refocus our perspective about what an authentic church does. Let's undermine all the bad memories by asking, Did you ever meet a real Christian? Did you ever enjoy the love of a church? Did you ever feel the warmth of Christian caring? Have you ever received forgiveness before you asked? Has the love of Christ ever constrained someone to befriend you in surprising, generous ways? Let's understand the truth as if it were flashing in neon lights: Nearly every positive influence in our society and nearly every hope have deep Christian roots. Even people who have never been influenced by the church have been enriched by Christian influence on public policy and by ethical demands in business, government, and family.

Creating Unforgettable Memories for Children

Try to remember what the church taught you in childhood that you are obligated to pass on. Into this exercise, factor the reality that many ideals and beliefs are eternal, though much has changed since your childhood. Use this short list to jog your list of influences you must pass on to those who come behind you.

Self-Worth

Growing up born again was sometimes hard to face in public school. School peers considered it strange if they knew someone was a devoted Christian, so I (Neil) sometimes experienced harassment on the playground or in the locker room. Kids loved to say, "Here comes holy Neil," "They do strange things at Neil's church," or "He goes to church in a house."

Though it was hard to understand then, I realize now their comments were sometimes expressions of curiosity. But how does a fourth grader decipher between belligerence and curiosity? What a difference between church and school. Church people treated me as an important family member. Some at church took me home to play with their children. Others helped me learn how to survive those hostile remarks at school. That happened naturally at church because each individual was valued as a person whom God loved enough to create and redeem. That's especially encouraging to know during those "Who am I?" identity years. That positive input was so much different from what I received from the gruff school counselor, who advised me in the seventh grade, "Don't count on going beyond high school because you're not college material."

Simple Faith

I (Neil) was wonderfully drawn to the Savior when an invitation was given in a regular service. Though the minister's invitation was primarily directed to adults, children were not excluded. When I responded, my Sunday school teacher introduced me to a simple faith in Christ. She told me about Jesus, the Friend of children. She spoke of a God of acceptance, love, and understanding who knew me better than I knew myself.

Even through seminary and other graduate studies, my heart has frequently been drawn back to the simple, sensible faith my Sunday school teacher helped me discover. The formation of faith planted by that teacher still enriches my life. It still shows in my ministries to my generation and the next and the next. I can still hear the children in that little Sunday school singing,

Jesus loves the little children, all the children of the world.
Red and yellow, black and white, they are precious in His sight.
Jesus loves the little children of the world.

Maybe what I felt then is what Jesus meant when He said, "Unless you are converted and become as little children, you will by no means enter the kingdom of heaven" (Matt. 18:3). These remembrances make me feel close to my spiritual roots planted by that little church of my childhood.

Facing Death

My parents lost a full-term baby girl at birth, probably because of incompetent medical care. I (Neil) was an only child, a ten-year-old. I remember that troubling time, and I wondered where God was. It was a critical moment for my faith development. I had no idea how to deal with death; I could not comprehend the loss of a baby. Our biological extended family did everything they could do. All the funeral customs of our culture were faithfully followed. But I remember most the family of God showing us love, and I remember how they spoke with assurance about the resurrection of Jesus that makes us victors over our fear of the grave. Even more, I remember their visits to our home, their hugging me, their talking to me, and their praying with us.

Living Faith in Relationships

The core of Christianity, according to Christ, is to love the Lord with the whole self and to love our neighbors as ourselves. That's a big order requiring a combination of divine enablement and human hard work. The first-century disciples demonstrated it so well. This love in a church is like love in a family that can be communicated through loving deeds without a single word being said. Living in love among the people of God is sometimes tough, requiring high standards of behavior and authentic accountability. But I (Neil) learned in church that one could think differently from another and still not break fellowship with that person. We might even wish another would refrain from certain actions without withholding our love.

Once our little church had an awful fuss. Hot words burned and bruised. Our family decided we would move to a nearby congregation to find peace and harmony. On Sunday morning when we left home for church, my father turned the car toward the old church rather than the new church. My mother was puzzled and asked, "Where are you going? I thought we were going to a new church today." My dad replied, "I can't do it. We'll have to find a way to work it out." As a Christian under construction, about twelve years old, I learned a lot from that incident.

Serving Others

The servanthood of Jesus provides a pattern for discovering great fulfillment. So much needs to be done in the church—from praying to painting, singing to serving, cutting the grass to shoveling the snow, and traditions to teaching. Since the list is almost endless, there is a place for everyone to serve. Many churches do everything for children, which is a mistake if we want to raise well-balanced children to Christian adulthood. Children need something to do that needs to be done.

A church in greater Los Angeles once a month takes a group of nine- to eleven-year-olds to serve food to homeless people at the Los Angeles Mission. I once watched them serve an evening meal; homeless people reached out to the children and the kids beamed with pride. Everyone gained something wonderful in that relationship.

Doing acts of service in Jesus' name helps children form a cornerstone for a life of meaning; fulfillment in life is multiplied by serving others. Robert Coles, the Harvard specialist on the spirituality of children, tells about a young African-American college student who put himself at risk as a civil rights activist. Later Coles asked the student, "Why do you keep at this, given the danger and the obstacles?" The student gave this surprising answer, "The satisfaction, man, the satisfaction."[1] That's a lesson to learn in church.

In a world needing spiritual reformation, the church can become a much more effective change agent as it teaches its young that it is in serving that they will be served and in giving that they receive. Serving is an effective spiritual vaccination against raising another "me-first" generation.

Belonging

The traditions of the church help children feel they belong and produce predictability in a time of rapid change. In *Fiddler on the Roof,* Tevye says, "Because of our traditions, everyone knows who he is and what God expects him to do."[2] In the church of my (Neil's) childhood we had many traditions—Christmas caroling including every age, watchnight services on New Year's Eve to commit to making the new year Christ-centered, Easter sunrise services to celebrate the Resurrection, and Easter and Christmas programs with memorized recitations by every child. Traditions put children in touch with the past even as they observe contemporary role models of the Christian faith. Rituals and ceremonies help children feel connected to their own families at church as well as the historic church and give them opportunity to participate.

Extended Family

Since the church is sometimes closer in spirit, geography, and interest than our extended biological family, it provides "uncles" and "aunts" and "grandparents" and "cousins" and "brothers" and "sisters." A church family childhood friend once told my wife, Bonnie Wiseman, "It's amazing how old I was before I realized we weren't actually related."

As an extended family, persons in our church felt responsible for others whenever needs arose. Once I (Neil) was disciplined at home after I told my parents that my Sunday school teacher had to discipline me at church—two punishments for the same offense. For us, the church provided an extended family who believed in us and loved us.

Though these recollections are set in an earlier time, to-day kids in rural, urban, and suburban settings need regular one-on-one relationships with caring adults. Children need sustained relationships with adults who feel privileged to show interest in their spiritual well-being.

Your Personal Growth Points

Every reader has a favorite way of remembering how a church shaped him or her. Which of the values you received from church can you pass on? What new values should be added? What will you imprint on the next generation that they will feel obligated to share with the next generation?

The more high tech our society becomes, the more people will feel a need for friendship, intimacy, acceptance, and a place to belong. That's what the church can provide. There people are shaped into greatness by Christ-exalting relationships. But let's get it right. Large masses of people feel overprogrammed by demands to upgrade their skills at work, by their community or civic responsibilities, by school activities, and by professional travel. Thus, they do not feel the need for more church programs, but they often find lots of time to be with people who will stretch them to become spiritually whole persons.

Let's influence children so that they can never get the Father and the church out of their minds or their hearts. Then they will be forever spoiled from enjoying a God-empty life; then they will point their own children and grandchildren to Christ.

NOTES

1. Robert Coles, *The Call of Service* (Boston: Houghton Mifflin, 1993), 69.

2. As quoted in *Current Thoughts & Trends,* February 1996, 12.

Chapter 11

Tribute to the Folks on Dubay Street

The Power of Spiritual Roots

Long before Detroit's inner city turned into a social jungle with killings on busy corners, crack houses in formerly quiet neighborhoods, drive-by shootings that kill innocent children, wholesale automobile factory closings, and unbelievable residential and business property decay, a little boy was nurtured there by a village of Christ-saturated people. The village was actually a tiny community of faith within a great city, living proof that Jesus' teaching about salt and light works. Though Motor City's population numbered two million or more at the time, the little congregation lived mostly within a two-mile radius of one another on the east side of the city near the end of the old city airport runway. In a sense, they were an island of faith within the larger population mass.

Folks in that little house church, located in the middle of a residential block, loved one another, especially children, and became a caring extended family to a newly married teenage couple and their baby son, Neil. The little congregation—seldom numbering more than ninety—consisted mostly of blue-collar workers who moved to the city to seek employment in automobile factories. From the beginning, the community of caring believers offered life-changing faith to children of the community. No one seems to remember whether the founders' original plan was to plant a church or to teach the Bible to neighborhood boys and girls. But it became a church nonetheless.

To those who were forever influenced by that small group of people, the beginning was a miracle of grace. Those whose lives were shaped there believe the house church was providentially placed in that setting so they could be loved to Christ by an extended church family.

The story of the Dubay church's beginning cannot be understood apart from two Sunday school women who wanted to teach the Bible to neighborhood children. Mrs. Healy and Mrs. Hoefler—sorry, but I can't recall their first names because children never addressed adults that way in those days—began Sunday afternoon Bible classes for children in their living rooms. Depending on weather conditions, they sometimes met on their front porches or in their backyards. There's a strong possibility that the founding women intended for the Bible classes only to provide a way to introduce their own children to Christ.

Whatever their intentions, they were not exclusive about who attended. In fact, they were aggressively inclusive with their invitation to neighborhood children. They taught everyone, regardless of age, in one class. They worked hard to invite new children every week—one boy started attending after being invited every week over a year's time. In response to such God-inspired persistence, this twelve-year-old boy started attending the Bible classes.

Then, in a few years when he married at nineteen and his bride was only sixteen, it was natural for them to attend the little church that had grown out of the beginning Bible classes he attended when he was twelve. The teachers were already some of his best adult friends. Today, we might call those teachers faith mentors. Though they had no name for what they did, they loved kids and showed it.

To share details of our tribute to the folks on Dubay Street, listen in on a conversation between H. B. and Neil.

HBL: Tell me about the facilities of the Dubay Church.

NBW: To a child who was first taken to the church at two weeks of age, the facilities seemed large and adequate. But memory has a way of making things bigger and better than they really were. The church was, in fact, a cement-block row house crowded into the middle of a city block. The entire first floor, along with an overflow porch, was used for a sanctuary. As needed, the worship area was divided with curtains that looked like bedsheets into spaces for youth and adult Sunday school classes. Those same white sheets were also used for stage curtains for Christmas and Easter pageants—the pageants had angels dressed in gaudy home-made white garments with glittering cardboard wings, and Christmas shepherds were always dressed in oversized, borrowed wool bathrobes.

HBL: Talk to me about the people who attended the house church on Dubay and about church leaders.

NBW: Everyone knew everyone. All were expected to attend every service—if you were absent, someone checked following the service to be sure you were not ill or losing interest. I guess it was actually informal accountability, but no one knew to call it that. It was friends caring for friends in the name of Jesus.

The lay leaders had places of elected responsibility, but it was like persons who pass out presents at birthday parties—the titles and elections to office were no big deal. We were family—God's family—so all worked together. When one was inadequate or unprepared or feeling down, others stepped in to help. We worshiped together, ate together, talked together, cleaned the church together, and did Christmas caroling at neighborhood bars and shut-ins' homes together. We took turns furnishing the coal from our own basements one winter so the church could have heat.

We were a big happy family—we knew everybody's business and they knew ours. Many of the children attended the same schools. Sometimes we had old-fashioned family fights, too. Then when death took one of our number, we used Miller's Funeral Home, bought funeral wreaths from Van Maele's Florists, and buried our dead at Forest Lawn cemetery just across the fence from Lynch School.

Lay leaders were a lot like heads of clans who led because somebody had to do it and because the church family wanted them to do it. It was like stepping forward and offering to do some function or service such as an older brother does in an extended family. The church was togetherness to the max.

HBL: Who were the pastors that impacted your faith development as a child?

NBW: Two stand out even now: Patience Hole and Robert North. I love the memory of Pastor Patience Hole. A mother in Zion to us, she was a woman about ten years older than my parents who loved us into greatness. She expected us to be good Christians, so we stretched to what she expected. She thought we could be spiritually great, so we became more like Christ.

Pastor Hole, along with her husband—a produce peddler who ran his business from the back of his truck—and her little girl, lived in a basement apartment in the church on Dubay Street. Though she was a competent person, her love and simple piety influenced us most. She cared for the spiritual needs of her flock like a loving mother cares for her newborn baby. No need for her to worry about women's liberation issues; she was pastor and spiritual leader because of who she was in her relationship to Christ and to us.

The congregation respected and loved her. She touched our lives with the gospel. She lived the Christ-filled life before us. Like Jesus in the Incarnation, she identified with us in every possible way, and she was a part of our lives at births, deaths, holy Communion, baptism, job losses, and health problems. The small resources of money and limited facilities of the church didn't keep her from leading the family of God to care for each other and to share their faith with other children in the neighborhood. Without getting overly emotional about the relationship, she was an example of what the writer of Hebrews spoke about, "Of whom the world was not worthy" (Heb. 11:38). By her love and life, she taught us devotion, acceptance, compassion, faithfulness, and authenticity. I often chuckle when I think about her name because she really needed patience to lead that little company of believers.

A self-made pastor, Robert North came in my preteen years. The church had grown some by the time he arrived and had moved to a converted bank building on the corner of VanDyke and Knodell. The building was easy to purchase because it had failed as a bank during the Great Depression and now had limited use. I remember working with the men of the church to tear out the old bank vault so we could have space for worship.

By calling Pastor North a self-made man, I mean he had no opportunities for formal education, but he educated himself. He studied hard, observed life, and trained himself to be an effective, loving pastor. Being a pastor was really a second career for him—he quit the factory to become a minister.

No one knows how he could afford to serve our church with a family of five children. It's still a mystery. But he did. His family was an important part of the families of the church, so his wife and children were included in most events. Singing at church, picnics in the park, social gatherings following burial of our people, church sports, attendance at revival meetings, worship at church, Sunday school classes, Christmas programs, prayer meetings—almost anything you can think of that could be done at church was part of their family agenda. Five children meant that nearly every Sunday school class had one of their children in the class. The family modeled what a home centered on Christ could be like. In many ways, their family taught us as much about Christ as did their father's preaching.

Pastor North taught us liberality, steadfastness, trust, and faith. In this close-knit community of faith, we learned to face life and accept death. We learned to love troubled people, rehabilitate dysfunctional families, provide food for needy people, serve homeless people in the city's rescue missions, care for one another in bad economic times, cherish children as the hope of the future, and nurse spiritually battered people back to wholeness. I love to think of those times as a beautiful human mosaic of service to others. If you needed something, the church tried to provide it.

HBL: It sounds almost too idealistic, something like a church for the Cleavers in a time and place when everything was right.

NBW: Sorry to leave that impression. Times have changed. I know we can't re-create those former days. I don't want to. Our situation was far from ideal, as most situations are. Our people had frequent layoffs with almost no public assistance. Coming out of the Great Depression, many of our people worked for the WPA—a government work program. Then came World War II when housewives left their homes for work and young men went away to fight a war. One or two of our number were killed in action. Grown children disappointed their parents. Children sometimes ran away from home. One or two of us were suspended from school. It was not ideal, but it was a relationship where we shared grace in difficulties.

Sometimes, it seemed everyone in our church was in crisis because everyone's problems were our own problems. We prayed for one another. We supported one another spiritually, emotionally, and sometimes economically. Perhaps the church was so influential in our lives because circumstances were bad.

As I think about it, I know it was not the programs of the church that shaped me—it was the people. And they were not perfect or special or wonderfully gifted—sometimes they were not any of those. They simply attempted to live out the spirit of Christ in their relationships with one another, and generally, they succeeded. When people fell, as they sometimes did, the community of faith gathered around them, loved them, offered them a lift, and urged them to try again. Often we saw grace most at work in incredible imperfections of people.

HBL: Were new children and their families welcomed there?

NBW: Oh, yes. During my childhood years in that church, I learned the church is one of the few places where troubled, even dysfunctional, families can find help and healing. I'm convinced many dysfunctional families are attracted to a caring church just because they have never experienced an extended family that would love them regardless of what they have done or who they are. It is unconditional love—what theologians call *agape* love.

Think about it. Many social problems faced by society have some solution in the church. Such accepting love cannot be found anywhere else in our society. Of course, not all churches provide an ideal sense of extended family, but a church can and it should. God expects it and even provides the enablement to make it possible. It is a spirit and priority and way of life more than a method or procedure or strategy. For two thousand years, the love of Christ has motivated and energized people to care for children. It still works today. And when they experience it, children and their parents treasure that love.

HBL: I'm nervous about what sounds too good to be true. How can a church touch an individual child when the contemporary agenda seems to be building bigger buildings, developing more programs, and being a religious business rather than a spiritual, extended family?

NBW: My tribute to the Dubay folks is intended to help people realize that ministry to a child may involve programs, buildings, big budgets, and large staffs. But it can also be the work of ordinary people in small, out-of-the-way places. Though I can't prove it, I suspect that most Christian leaders came from such a setting.

The first step is to realize that the potential of every child provides an opportunity for a church to enrich the life of that child. Serving and loving one child may even impact the future of the nation and shape generations yet unborn. Anyone can take the spirit of Christ into children's lives, and the payoff happens when members of the next generation center their lives on what Christ wants for their families, businesses, and governments.

Today in every church, you will find children who will tomorrow head families, be community leaders, or work in a secular setting that desperately needs the influence of

Christ. Right now in some churches, there is a future Mother Teresa, a future Chuck Colson, a future James Dobson, or a future Ordinary Joe.

Think, too, about children who need what the church offers but who never experience it. Without the influence of Christ, down the street or around the corner from many churches are potential killers and shocking social misfits. Like children everywhere, these people offer us a narrow window of opportunity in which to introduce them to Christ so they can learn about the most wonderful way to live that has ever been discovered. That way is to follow Christ and to seek to be like Him. But many children will never know about it unless we tell them.

HBL: Can you tell me specifically what the little house church on Detroit's Dubay Street did for you? Is there something reproducible that every church can do for its children, regardless of the church's size, location, or doctrine?

NBW: Let me offer a quick list that any church can do without spending a dollar:

- Love children, and let them know it.
- Introduce children to Jesus as their Friend.
- Love every child as if you were showing love to Christ.
- Give time to children and become their adult friend.
- Don't wait until everything is perfect to start; sophisticated programs are not nearly as important as loving hearts.
- Understand that children will be forgiving of mistakes.
- Work with confidence that faith is caught as well as taught.
- Do not be intimidated by those who try to make you believe contemporary government programs take the place of a loving church.

- Teach parents that faith development is fully as important as good nutrients for children.
- Be quick to show the compassion of Christ to children who are in family crises. You may be their only hope.

HBL: Before we finish, I suppose you want to tell your story about how my preacher grandfather impacted your life.

NBW: I was afraid you would never ask. I joke lots of times that your grandfather almost ruined my faith. But before I begin, why don't you introduce your grandfather to our readers. He knew the awesome, eternal value of touching children with the love of Christ.

HBL: My grandfather was a Sunday school evangelist who traveled from church to church, helping congregations double their Sunday schools over a two- or three-week period. His plan was to preach inspiration to the people and then organize them for a big Sunday school rally day on the last Sunday of the revival. The process was to increase the church's impact on families in the community, starting with those who lived closest to the church. Usually, the campaigns lasted for three Sundays, and church services were held each night in between. In those days, guest preachers usually stayed in people's homes, so evangelists and church members sometimes became well acquainted over a two-week period.

Granddad's goal was to help a church see its potential, and that included children. He believed a combination of organization, hard work, and inspiration would produce new people. He and Grandmother sang together in revivals, so the music, his inspirational preaching, and his practical plan made him effective. In many places, the churches actually doubled their Sunday school attendance for the closing Sunday school rally. Can you imagine the excitement that caused? His ministry fit his times exactly, and he had a full schedule. For many years, I often heard people say, "We had our largest Sunday school attendance ever when Dr. A. S. London was here as our evangelist!"

NBW: That's a great introduction—almost too lofty a way to start my story. But I still love to tell it.

At the little house church on Dubay Street, your grandfather came as evangelist when Pastor Patience Hole was our minister. The incident took place on a dark, cold Michigan November night—a night when only the faithful would consider attending church. So the crowd was down, and your grandfather was trying to impress his hearers with the kingdom value of every child. I was four years old and sound asleep during most of the service—that is, until he woke me. In a moment of inspiration, your grandfather grabbed me, held me high over his shoulder, and shouted at the top of his voice, "How much is this boy worth?" It was a hard, demanding question to ask anyone, and he knew it.

But can you imagine what that did to me—an unforgettable question comes booming into your consciousness when you are a sleepy four-year-old? I felt as though I was in the midst of a thousand nightmares combined. I love to remind you, H. B., that your grandfather almost ruined my faith, and who knows how much he damaged my psyche that night.

However, A. S. London's intention when he used me as a living illustration for his sermon is exactly what we mean when we say it takes a church to really raise a child. Dr. London's question still rings in my ears. His question still makes me think about my relationship to children. His question makes me look at children in church and department stores and playgrounds and parks. His question makes me wonder about the potential of every child I meet.

His question makes me ask myself serious questions about who really influences children for Christ. His question makes me ask hard questions about the church I attend. His question makes me ask searching questions about what I did spiritually for my children when they were at home and what I can do to build faith in their children and their children's children.

His question is as up to date as the horrible problems that affect contemporary children. Hear it again: How much is this boy worth? If the boy is your boy or the girl is your girl, the answer is, *He or she is worth everything.*

Let's ask and answer that question in every family, in every community, in every church, and in every school. A nation or society that neglects its children is on its way to rapid havoc and eventual ruin. How much is this child worth? How much will we work and how much will we pay to make him or her spiritually, emotionally, and physically whole? HOW MUCH IS EVERY CHILD WORTH?

Chapter 12

39 WAYS TO IMPROVE OUR IMPACT ON CHILDREN
You Can Make a Difference

It's time to think about specific ways to strengthen ministry to children in every church in the land. Foundation to everything else must be our preaching and teaching about God's view of the human family and of the family of God—His church. That means we stress the significance of the biological family. That means we keep before our congregations the disastrous consequences our society and individuals can expect from anything less than a Christ-centered church and healthy family relationships.

It's time to counteract all the harm society, the media, and so-called political correctness do to undermine family values and destroy innocent children. With every ounce of holy energy that God gives us, we must fight the idea that alternative family lifestyles are simply acceptable replacements for the way God intends us to live. The destructive consequences of alternative family structures must be shown for what they really are. This communication must be so clear that persons who consider divorce will know from our earlier ministries to them that they are setting themselves up for problems that are larger than the ones they have. This communication must be so efficient that teens know the consequences of premarital sex, including pregnancy, a bad conscience, death, or undermining for years the sexual adjustments of their eventual marriage. This communication must be so efficient that members of the church know how vital righteousness is in their parenting. This communication must be so efficient that everyone in the church has a clear idea of what we are doing to our children this very day. But how do we do that and do it well?

1. *Use God's values to counter secular values.* We can do this in our preaching, teaching, and living. A veteran country preacher said, "It is not only good to be a Christian, but it is also smart." Let's tell it well: Real Christians live happier, more fulfilled lives than people who choose to live their lives according to the patterns and values of the secular society. The Christian lifestyle is the most fulfilling way to live that anyone has ever discovered. We need to speak up about the Ten Commandments being a great way to live. Pastors can underscore the distinctions between scriptural and secular views of marriage, family, and child rearing as they conduct marriage ceremonies, dedicate or baptize infants, do pastoral counseling, and informally interact daily with members of the congregation.

2. *Model healthy Christian families.* Invest time, effort, and money in making your family an example of what healthy families can be. The modeling is desirable and convincing to others, but the real payoff is the joy and satisfaction you receive from doing it. This effort is not just for families with young children at home. It can be modeled in grown families, empty nesters, and golden agers, too.

3. *Build your church into a support system.* When children are threatened or abused, when marriages are stressed, when teenagers rebel, the church can become a support system for hurting people. It can also become a place where

fractured lives can be put back together again after the storm subsides.

4. Organize a mentoring system for children. Here's an incredibly powerful way one contemporary church builds extended family relationships in its fellowship. Miles McPherson and Wayne Rice tell about a multiracial, inner-city congregation with a burden for reaching teens who have few positive adult role models in their lives. The youth leaders recruit adult church members as mentors to teach young people life skills. Another group of mentors in the same church periodically takes teens to work so the youths can see how responsible Christians earn a living. And another group of adults adopts teens as prayer partners.[1] Responsible, Christ-motivated adults will grow spiritually strong out of this mentoring relationship even as the teens grow. The congregation's vision is that someone out of this group of teens will make a startling difference in urban problems in the next generation.

5. Look to Scripture for answers. In all areas of ministry, take the clear teachings from Scripture about children and family life, and make sure everyone understands them and also understands how to apply them to their family relationships.

6. Practice perseverance and prevention as well as redemption. Aspire magazine reports, "Couples who attend church together have the lowest risk of divorce, according to researchers at Brigham Young University. However, if only one spouse attends, the couple has a higher likelihood of splitting up than if they both stayed home. People with no religious affiliation have a higher divorce rate than those who marry someone of a different faith or denomination."[2] The church must provide better teaching and information and motivation about sound, wholesome family life. Marriage encounters, family life conferences, and family caucuses should be offered. Of course, the church must always be there to offer new lives for old for those who have allowed sin to blight their lives, but it must also do better with keeping the blight from infecting Christian families.

7. *Aid broken families, especially the children.* We must come alongside adults and children from broken families so they can see ways to begin to rebuild their lives in an environment of love and understanding rather than in an environment of isolation and alienation.

8. *Cherish children on all levels of church life.* When we serve children, we have their futures in our hearts and our hands. There is something wonderful about being able to shape lives that will be having an influence in our world after we are gone. Our present situation is desperate. We're talking life and death. We're talking about children being disabled emotionally and spiritually for life. We're talking about kids never knowing a stable family life. We're talking about children who have no idea of the value of human life. We're talking about a world where gunfire is the second leading cause of death among Americans ages ten to nineteen—where a child is killed every ninety-two minutes by gunfire.[3]

9. *Insist on family purity among leaders.* Some churches, with a notion of tolerance, have allowed leaders to be less pure than the general population. God will not stomach such sinfulness. A very sexually mixed-up young adult told one of us in a counseling situation, "One of the reasons I am so messed up is because of the Peyton Place stuff I saw in the church where I grew up—nearly everyone had a sexual hang-up, and we all knew about it." That cannot be allowed. God expects church leaders to be pure and chaste, and He provides enablement to live such a life.

10. Carry placards and write letters. Lead your church to influence political leaders who draft and vote on community, state, and national policy. Be firm, be sensible, be Christian, and carry the ball for children who have few lobbyists to speak for them.

11. Train yourself to view children by their potential. It's easy to see how present negative trends in our society will produce negative results in children. On the contrary, we can predict positive spiritual results with children. The twelve- and thirteen-year-olds in your present youth group will be heads of families in fifteen to twenty years. What kinds of families will they head?

12. Align the family of God and the human family. They are the two last bastions for meaning and righteousness. Pastor Richard Dobbins says it well: "The natural family was designed by God to procreate, nurture, strengthen, and sustain life from birth to death. In much the same way, the church, as the spiritual family of God, has been designed to evangelize, nurture, discipline, strengthen, and sustain the life of God's children."[4] Try to see family issues as being directly related to the mission of the church.

Years ago, in an article in *Religion in Life,* Samuel L. Hamilton said, "The church cannot function as she should in a disordered world unless she employs the home as her main reliance in Christian nurture. And I feel certain that the family cannot be a Christian family or a happy family unless it stays in the circulation of those spiritual influences of which the church is the greatest custodian."[5] That's still true.

13. Resource the home. We must continually avoid the temptation to let the church attempt to provide all of the Christian training children receive. Because of the relatively small amount of time children spend at church, it cannot be done even if they are involved in everything the church provides including Sunday school, vacation Bible school, weekend club/Bible study, and children's church. The discouraging dilemma is that in our time many parents do not know how to give their children Christian training. They will never learn how to do it without purposeful attempts by the church to teach them.

14. Maintain strong outreach contacts with unchurched families. Ministering to children without trying to spiritually impact their families is like placing Band-Aids on the fissures caused by an earthquake. Parents are often more open to a church's outreach efforts than we think. Our church planter friend Jim Dorsey has organized a church in Rancho Santa Margarita, California, called the Family Church— "where you'll feel right at home." A mass mailer from his church communicates this idea in a headline that reads, "At first we went for our children; now we go to church for all of us." The ad copy continues,

> Perhaps you are like a lot of concerned parents—looking for a place for your family to develop spiritually and learn more about God. If you've given up on church or consider yourself a "non-church goer," you'll be in good company. Over 70 percent of our congregation describe themselves that way. At least they did before they started attending the Family Church. Come and check out this young and growing congregation some Sunday morning at 10:00—you owe it to yourself and your family.

Think of all parents of children who come to church alone as prospects who need your church. Focus the church on reaching out to them in every possible way; they have already trusted you with their most prized possessions.

15. Avoid overscheduling. Age-group activities at the church nurture children, but they must be balanced against the need for family time. Some churches do not schedule church activities at least one or two nights each week, and they encourage church families to use those evenings as times for togetherness and nurture.

16. Provide family-together activities. More and more families, especially those that live a great distance from their extended families, need church activities—ministries and events that include two or more generations. Examples might include all-church fellowship activities where families eat together, church services where family members attend and sit together, musical programs where people from all generations are asked to participate, or cross-generational craft activities. Some churches do outreach calling in family units so the children and early teens are part of the ministry. Another church has two or three families call together on older people who cannot leave their homes and on residents of nursing facilities.

17. Establish parenting support groups. The idea is to network parents with other parents who are facing the same issues in child rearing. These training times present information and help parents sharpen their parenting skills. In the support groups, people are also encouraged to share their experiences and to express their love and support for one another. Here's a starter topic list:

- Caring for newborns
- Dealing with TV's impact on kids
- Matching family devotions to a child's development
- Coping with strong-willed children
- Applying the Bible to the child's life
- Modeling faith at home

18. Inform parents about what is being taught at church.
Sunday school teachers can do this by periodically sending
notes to each home and explaining what lessons are being
studied. Notices can be placed in the bulletin and newsletter
about what is being covered in Sunday school. Encourage
parents to visit their children's Sunday school class. Have a
special reception for parents and children like a parent-
teacher conference in the public schools.

19. Provide support to parents of rebellious children. Often
the rebellion of a child has to be borne all alone by parents.
They suffer grief about their loss of relationship. They feel
like failures. Many different voices tell them what to do—
some advise "put them out"; some advise "let them do what
they want"; some advise "they were born bad." It's a tough
road to travel, and most parents who face it have no experience to fall back on.

A pastor in training has a rebellious sixteen-year-old son
who was locked up for a serious crime. The boy refuses to
go to school, and last week his girlfriend (age fifteen) announced that she was expecting his child. That family needs
support and understanding and prayers and comfort. The
church needs to be there with whatever help it can offer.
Among the not-so-obvious fringe benefits of this effort is
that the other children in the family of the rebellious teen
will often remember all their lives with appreciation what
that church did for their family during difficult days.

20. Upgrade your children's Christian education programs.
In the technological revolution that is taking place in education, children sometimes have state-of-the-art educational
experiences at school and horse-and-buggy experiences at
church. Though the church many not be able to do everything to improve Christian education of children, it should
provide the best program it can afford.

The positive benefits children receive from first-rate Christian educational programs include Bible study at their level of understanding, interaction with other children in a Christian setting, opportunities to build Christian friendships in their age-group, and interaction and modeling of nonfamily Christian adults. Children learn teamwork and cooperation, and they experience Christian worship.

21. Intentionally build relationships with children in the community. Consider these approaches for starters: preschool, mother's day out, day care, tutorial programs, study hall at church until parents come from work, English as a second language, soccer camp, basketball camp, and day camping. One inner-city church opened up a whole new interest for the church in its community by installing basketball goals on the church parking lot and allowing neighborhood children to use them.

22. Implement annual prayer summits to pray for children. Do this once each year, on a Sunday evening, a weekday evening, or a Saturday morning. It can be interfaced with other ministries to children—for example, the week before vacation Bible school or church camp. The summit should probably be no more than three hours in length. Everyone who attends should be given a list of children's names for whom to pray. Sometime during the summit, conditions in which children live in your setting should be discussed. Teachers who serve in the public schools should be prayed for.

Before the summit closes, you may want the group to pray especially for divine guidance about what the Lord wants them to do for children. You may want to include in the prayer concerns that children may fear the Lord and serve Him (Deut. 6:13), know God personally early in life (2 Chron. 34:1–3), hate sin (Ps. 97:10), have a responsible attitude in all personal relationships (Rom. 13:8), desire the right kind of friends (Prov. 1:10, 15), and trust the Lord for direction in their lives (Prov. 3:5–6).

23. Provide mandatory and effective premarital counseling. This is part of the prevention and preservation effort for good marriages and is a background for raising strong Christian children. Some time ago, Jeannette and Robert Lauer did a study called "Marriages Made to Last." They interviewed three hundred couples married for fifteen years or longer. They asked couples to select from thirty-nine statements the ones that best showed why their marriages lasted. Here are some of the high-choice responses:

- My spouse is my best friend.
- I like my spouse as a person.
- Marriage is a long-term commitment.
- Marriage is sacred.
- We agree on aims and goals.
- My spouse has grown more interesting.
- I want the relationship to succeed.
- An enduring marriage is important to social stability.
- We laugh together.[6]

Couples should be helped to build these issues into their approaching marriages as part of a church's prevention effort to provide stable homes for future children.

24. Recruit couples for teaching and sponsorship assignments. The idea is to get families involved in working with kids and other families rather than just one person. Children see how Christian couples relate to each other—an important part of Christian training for nonchurch kids.

25. Avoid the fatigue of the faithful. Often a church overworks its most diligent members, so they live on the edge of burnout. Often they need more pastoral care than they receive. Often they need to spend more time developing relationships with their families. Overly tired people cannot be good role models to children.

26. Develop small groups. Two of the most popular types are support groups and growth groups. Every bookstore has material on how to organize small groups. To use Charles Swindoll's words, small groups are "the part that touches people by bringing the gospel up close."[7] George Whitefield, the great statesman of Methodism, said, "None that truly loves his own soul and his brethren as himself, will be shy of opening his heart in order to have their advice, reproof, admonition and prayer, as occasion requires. A sincere person will esteem it one of the greatest blessings."[8]

27. Experiment with intergenerational ministries. The purpose is to allow children to become friends with adults and adults to become friends with children—opportunities to cherish and learn from one another. A good way to start is to plan a program similar to the learning components that might take place in a third- or fourth-grade Sunday school class—storytelling, crafts, songs, maybe some action choruses. Divide your group into smaller groups of five or six people that include persons from three generations who are not related to one another. In one church each group studied the biblical story about Joseph's coat of many colors, and then each group made a coat out of paper gowns like those used in physicians' offices.

One church had a program where younger teens were responsible for attending the senior citizens' Christmas party, and each teen was to make friends with one golden ager. Before the meeting was over, there were duets and solos and trios of Christmas carols, and both age-groups were talking about what a good time they had. Family

church camping would be another opportunity for intergenerational impact.

28. Arrange adopt-a-kid family camping. An intact Christian family could adopt a child from an unchurched home
for the camp. Or the church might form weekend extended
family groups with single people in the church and the children whose families do not attend church. The whole idea is
to live out an extended family experience so every child has
at least one adult to whom he or she feels close at church.

29. Provide sex education at church. In many places,
church people have criticized public schools for offering sex
education. The arguments maintain public schools do not
teach Christian values about sexuality, family, and parenting. The objections also say this education should be left to
the home and the church. After these arguments are made
and accepted, the imperative is for the home and the church
to move into this area to teach values. The only problem is
that parents usually need help to know how, and the church
is about the only place they can get that help.

30. Conduct parenting classes. These classes should teach
Christian parenting skills. Such classes could be conducted
by effective Christian parents whose children are now
grown. Above all, be sure that everyone understands that
parenting is not a perfect art, but it is a learning laboratory
where people exercise understanding, love, forgiveness, and
acceptance. Most parents we know need assurance about
their parenting: New parents worry that they are doing it
wrong, parents of third graders worry that they are doing
it wrong, and people in their eighties worry that they did it
wrong with children who are now in their fifties.

31. Absorb singles into the family of God. When we talk
with singles, it soon becomes apparent that one of their biggest problems is feeling left out at church. Opening the

whole church to singles means they are included in elections, social activities, and committees, and involved in teaching ministries. Many churches would do a great service to children if singles were intentionally involved in children's ministries, something like a big brother or big sister program. Family specialist Charles Sell says, "When the church is like a family, singles can find the family that they need. They not only want involvement; they want close involvement."[9] Singles provide a magnificent source of workers for deepening a church's ministry to children.

32. Customize ministry to a particular child. When Barbara was left a widow with two boys, ages seven and nine, the men's fellowship in her small church decided they would help her raise the boys. From the men's group of only ten members, someone volunteered to do some man-type activity with them every month. Within a few months, the boys felt close to most of the men in the church. After two or three years, Barbara married again and moved away, but today her sons, now grown men, are actively looking after boys in the churches where they attend.

Consider the kids who need someone the most. Why not organize a plan to be sure they are cared for and cherished? As is the case for all Christian service activities, those who give may receive more than they gave.

33. Emphasize rituals. Weddings, baptisms, Communion services, and church membership receptions are all big events in the lives of participants. Make a big deal of the rituals, especially ones that involve children.

One church asks children ages eight and up to help pack Thanksgiving baskets for low-income people and people who cannot leave their homes. Another church has a Thanksgiving morning country breakfast where one adult does the cooking and the young teens do the serving. They even let the kids elect the layperson of the year and award a trophy to that person at the breakfast.

34. Institute or revitalize the children's sermon. A while ago, I (Neil) visited a famous old church in San Francisco where the worship style was so wild and the theology so liberal, I hardly knew I was in church. But when the time came for the pastor's sermon for children, he sat on the front of the platform and told the children about the love of God. I watched the children's eyes, and I could see that they adored their pastor. I also looked around and noticed that every adult in the congregation was carefully listening to the sermon intended for children. Interest level was stronger for the children's sermon than anything else that happened in that service. Church will mean something important to those children for the rest of their lives because of how close they obviously felt to their pastor. When some adults are asked about their warmest memories from childhood, they often describe a caring person who touched their lives at a special moment. Why not make that moment the pastor's sermon to children?

35. Make the church children friendly. If you were three feet tall and walked into your church, what would the church facilities say to you? What would your Sunday school room say to you? What impressions would you receive from people who greet you at the door? One pastor we know whose church has an attendance of about four hundred knows every child by name. He has dedicated many of them to Christ, and he plans to be their pastor when they are old enough to be elected to official decision-making groups. Another pastor joked, "Being nice to children is my job security for the future."

36. Provide family life skills training. Charles Sell provides a list of concerns that one congregation gave when they were asked what areas of training they were most interested in. Out of forty-five choices, here are their top ones: marriage enrichment, marriage communication, family communication, roles of husband and wife, teaching Christian values at home, parenting young children, marital conflict resolution, leading children to Christ, marital problem solving, finances and money management, and family worship—family spiritual time.[10]

The list might be different in your church, but the list indicates that people in the church wanted help with marriage issues, family issues, and spiritual development. One church determined to plan one family training event about every three months, so they had marriage enrichment weekends, how to get along with parents for teens, dads discipling dads, and marriage maintenance seminars.

37. Emphasize teen abstinence. Since the church knows there are significant benefits resulting from sexual purity and sexual abstinence before marriage, a program like the Southern Baptist "True Love Waits" should be considered by every church. Give this research some thought: "Calling it 'the most poignant finding of their study,' researchers writing in the *Journal of Youth and Adolescence* reported that 43 percent of sexually experienced teens wish they hadn't engaged in premarital intercourse."[11]

38. Hold a "What Is Needed?" forum. After reading this book and becoming more aware of the problems facing children and families, why not invite a group of ten or twelve people to a brainstorming session where you talk about the needs of children in your church? Make a list of the needs, and then think creatively in the group about how those

needs might be met with the existing facilities and personnel. Perhaps a mission search group could grow out of this
meeting where a group of people would commit to one another to meet for prayer and Bible study once each week
with the express purpose of determining how your church or
your group could better serve children. Some churches have
discovered great benefits from such a group meeting for
Bible study and prayer around the question, What does God
want us to do? Such prayer often provides a clear focus of a
need, the available resources, and helpful motivation for
getting started.

39. Put on "potential" glasses. I'll need a paragraph or two
to explain.

If you could see me (Neil) now as I finish the last pages
of this book, I have a tear in my eye and a bit of frustration
and hope in my heart. What a journey of discovery it has
been trying to think through these ideas and share them
with you!

I want to tell a story I read in a book called *Creating
Community*. I bought the book because I wanted to hear
what people outside the church thought community was and
what it should accomplish. When I got around to reading
the book, I discovered it was saturated with ideas about how
lonely people go about seeking community and how a sense
of community can be built, but I can't recall that it mentions
the church in 330 pages. I kept thinking as I read, community is the church's business. The church has been in the
fellowship and caring business for two thousand years.

Let me tell you still more about my frustration and about
my hope.

The book tells a powerful story about a sophisticated urban unmarried secularist who, at forty-two, found herself

eight months pregnant with her first child and deserted by the father, who told her in no uncertain terms he had no plans to continue living with her or supporting the child. Feeling all alone and terrified, she didn't know what to do.

However, at the moment where we meet her in the book, she is surrounded by about two dozen women, men, and children, giving her a baby shower. The gifts were the usual fare for baby showers, but they also brought a recycled stroller and baby buggy. And there was more. They promised to be with her during delivery, to help her bring the baby home from the hospital, to support her emotionally, to help with baby-sitting, and to stay in her life as much as possible until the baby was grown.

Then they assured her they counted it a priceless treasure to be able to have a part in her baby's life. Her patched-together family of friends gave her one loud and clear message: "We'll be here for you."

I wondered if the church would do a thing like that. I'm hopeful the church will someday, maybe soon, welcome every child with that kind of enthusiasm. Of course, we can't and won't approve of the sins of the parents, but as Jesus said, when we receive a child, it is as if we receive Him.

Thank You, Mrs. Frederick!

Could we move beyond doing our duty to children and see the possibilities, the hopes, and the newness that every child brings to the world, to the church, to the family, and the richness that comes to all who dare to be a part of the network of folks at church that help raise a child?

Another story needs telling to add balance to the picture of what the church can mean to kids. Let's let Linda Frederick tell the story in the first person:

I was running late one Sunday morning on the way to my primary class. I huffed my way downstairs to the children's department with my coat flapping and my arms full.

Suddenly, among the cheerful greetings I heard a deep masculine voice—"Wait up, Mrs. Frederick! Wait!" I paused and turned to see a young man, well over six feet tall, racing down the stairs after me. Something about him was vaguely familiar. "Do you remember me?" he asked. He looked rather timid, even though I had to bend my neck far back to look into his big brown eyes. "My name is Mark. Mark J—."

My mind tumbled back seven, eight—no, I realized it had been more than ten years ago. I recalled a dirty child wearing ragged tennis shoes and no socks in the middle of winter. Mark was sullen, angry, and ready to fight anyone, myself included, who got in his way. Abused and rejected by his parents, Mark had to live with his unwilling grandmother. As a respite from his rebellion and anger, she had forced him to get on the church bus.

"Yes, of course," I cried, "of course I remember you." I didn't explain why I remembered him. Mark laughed nervously, took my heavy box, and started downstairs. Plodding along behind him, I wondered what I would say to this boy I had known for such a short time. Despite the dirt, anger, and pathetic clothes, I had felt a special bond with him.

Setting down the box, Mark turned to me. There were tears in his eyes. "I came back to find you. I wanted to tell you how much you meant to me," he said softly. "In all my life you were the only one who ever really, deep down, loved me. No matter what happened to me, I knew that you were some place loving me. It helped a lot." Now there were tears in my eyes. Yes, I realized, I did still love him. Even though I had heard nothing from him during all those years, he did cross my mind.

"Could I hug you?" he asked suddenly. Forgetting I had a big class coming, not caring if I was prepared, I wrapped my arms around him and held on for all I was worth. With that, he was gone, waving and grinning broadly.

As Mark walked away, I couldn't help wondering if I had done all I could for him. I had loved him, despite himself. I had taught him the Word of God, making certain he understood his need for a Savior and the way to Christ. I had tried to meet his physical needs by providing some socks and a warm coat. Yes, I had done all I could.

I remembered being discouraged that Mark had rejected both Christ and me. Yet, this Sunday morning, God showed me that what had happened on the outside was not what was going on inside. Mark had remembered me, my love, and even my hugs. He said they helped him get through those ten silent years. The same love had driven him back to the church to find me. I couldn't help wondering if he also was searching for my God. Forgetting everything else, I bowed my head and prayed for the young man who had hurried away. "Please show him the way," I prayed. "Direct him to someone who will once again show him how he might become Your child!"

Who knows what lives will be changed by our faithful service? Who can say how many boys and girls will be part of God's kingdom because we are willing not only to teach a Sunday school class, but really love the boys and girls? As students filed into the room, I searched each face. I will teach them to the best of my ability and faithfully give them the Word of God and the plan of salvation. I will start this class—and every class—with a hug. After all, Mark said I can hug real good![12]

Our list of ways to serve children is only a beginning. But it is a start—a useful start, we hope. The specific steps of improved ministry to children are not nearly as important as your caring and loving and behaving. The most vital ministries to children generally start by people praying, "Oh, Lord, what can we do?" Start praying that prayer now, and God will impress you with a way to help in your field of work that is both possible and fun to accomplish. Go for it.

NOTES

1. Miles McPherson and Wayne Rice, "Replace Meetings with Mentors," *Youthworker,* fall 1995, 28.

2. *Aspire,* February 1996, as quoted in *Current Thoughts & Trends,* March 1996, 12.

3. *Gazette Telegraph* (Colorado Springs), April 9, 1996.

4. Richard D. Dobbins, *The Family Friendly Church* (Altamonte Springs, Fla.: Creation House, 1989), 97.

5. Samuel L. Hamilton, *Religion in Life,* summer 1949, 18.

6. Richard P. Olson and Joe H. Leonard, Jr., *A New Day for Family Ministry* (New York: Alban Institute, 1996), 94.

7. As quoted by Charles M. Sell, *Family Ministry* (Grand Rapids: Zondervan, 1995), 117.

8. Ibid., 118.

9. Ibid., 324.

10. Ibid., 356.

11. As quoted in *Current Thoughts & Trends,* April 1996, 10.

12. Linda Frederick Golz, "Thank You, Mrs. Frederick." Used by permission.

Epilogue

THE CHURCH FOR THE NEW GENERATION

This book has been dedicated to our grandchildren and to all of the children everywhere who will carry the mantle of Jesus Christ into the next millennium. On their behalf we offer these final words on the church we covet for them.

Taylor, Amanda, Hilary, Jeffrey, William, and Katie are the next generation of the Londons and Wisemans, and they are very important to us. We are sure that you could fill in the names of precious children in your life as well. Please know we're concerned about them, too.

When we think about children and their future in our kind of world, it's easy to forget the admonition of Scripture, "Be anxious over nothing." But we must not despair.

One of the great church leaders in the United States was asked how the future of the church looked to him. He turned to his inquirer and spelled out the word *Y-O-U-T-H*. He's right. The only hope for our world is for the church of Jesus Christ to build up children in the nurture and admonition of the Lord and for the church to invest its efforts in children everywhere—both inside and outside the church.

May I (H. B.) put my concerns for the next generation in first-person language.

When I was a young father and pastor, I took for granted that my children would be raised in a church family that would fill in the gaps Bev and I missed. Brad and Bryan, from their births, were loved by congregations we served. They had wonderful role models in youth leaders and other families in our churches. And we are grateful. And Neil and Bonnie feel the same about the way the churches they were privileged to lead loved their sons, Todd and Scott.

As I look back on those churches, especially during our sons' formative years, I am reminded they had activities that were positive and leaders who made them know they had worth and value. Today they are wonderful Christian husbands and fathers largely because of the influences of those churches on their lives. Were our children perfect? No way. They made as many mistakes as any other children make, but the churches loved them just the same. I know Bev and I made a lot of mistakes in raising our boys that we would reverse if we had the opportunity. Yet as we look back over the journey, we thank God for the family of God that helped us raise and influence our family.

What about today? What about the next generation? What should a church be, and how should a church set its priorities? Though the following thoughts are not scholarly or novel, they are things I covet for the new generation who will populate our churches in the years to come.

1. A church that is led by a faithful pastor. I want children to have a minister who is consistent and effective in his or her own family living and has a shepherd-servant spirit for everyone in the congregation. I want children to have a pastor who knows them by name, who cares about them, who takes time to listen. I want them to have a pastor whose messages are relevant and geared to real-life issues. I want children to have a pastor who loves them as Jesus loved the children He met along the way.

2. A church that is biblically based. I want a church for them where the essential truths of the Word of God are preached and practiced and where the Word of God determines the work of the church.

I want a church for them that will insist on the basic principles of morality as taught by Jesus in the Sermon on the Mount and one that takes seriously the admonition to live by the Ten Commandments. I want children to be encouraged to memorize and apply the Word of God to their lives.

3. A church that is financially generous. I want all children to have a church home where budgeting for the educational ministries for kids and young people has high priority. I covet that leaders will understand that to effectively teach and reach children and young people, they may have to make a much larger investment than they make in other ministries. Such an investment will pay off because the next generation will know they are loved, cared for, and valued by their church.

4. A church that trains parents. Today, parenting may be the most difficult assignment in the world. I realize we can't force-feed parents, but I also realize that every church needs a mentoring program whereby younger couples can identify with older, more established Christian families. This follows the teaching of 2 Timothy 2:2 where faithful men are commanded to teach what they have learned to the next generation.

5. A church that is served by dedicated laypersons. I know churches often need paid professionals as they grow larger. In reality only three churches in ten have more than one paid professional. But I want children to be influenced and loved by laypersons. Some of the most memorable moments in the church were those times when a lay leader loved me in spite of my faults and fears. They were wonderful people who loved God and felt called to walk alongside a young person. Granted, lay leaders need training, and the church needs to remember that the greatest fear anyone has when given ministry opportunities is the fear of not knowing how.

6. A church that teaches respect for authority. Authority that is based on scriptural principles—respect for the authority of parents, church, government, and educational system—is essential. Every young person needs to respect and look up to those to whom God has given direction to lead in the nation and the church. I want the next generation to know there are persons to whom God has given responsibility to watch over them and to give guidance to their lives.

7. A church that unapologetically confronts sin and injustice. I want the next generation to be confronted about their sins and given opportunity to confess, repent, and be forgiven. I want them to know it is never right or wise to rebel against God. I want someone to point out the danger of transgressions. I want the truth of the gospel presented to them at an early age so they can forsake their sins and develop the Christian lifestyle that God desires for them.

8. A church that teaches servanthood. We live in a complicated "me-oriented" society, and if a church does not provide its people opportunities to be "foot washers," it will rob them of a blessing. I hope the church will provide ways for the next generation to work in the inner city, to take missionary work trips, to assist older citizens, and to care for and help one another when difficulties come. I want them to experience what it means to come alongside another young person who is going through times of loneliness and failure. I want my grandchildren to have a church that will help them develop a heart like our Lord's.

9. A church that trains children and youths to recognize other Christians. I sincerely want them to learn that many genuine Christians do not see every detail of practice and belief in the same way. I hope my grandchildren will never feel superior to other people or think they are the only ones with an answer. I covet a church that will preach the truth, protect the absolute, and help the next generation make good spiritual choices, but never with an attitude of self-righteous superiority.

10. *A church that emphasizes a balanced lifestyle.* I want dedicated leaders to teach early that stewardship of time, talent, and treasure is as important as worship and attendance at church. I pray they are taught the value of tithing, giving of time in service to the body of Christ, and faithfully attending the services of worship.

11. *A church that stresses family values.* I realize that every home cannot have a mom and dad and biological children. Yet that traditional family can be the benchmark at which we begin. Our civilization cannot survive without stable homes. In this day when chastity and morality and fidelity are being denigrated, I covet a church for the next generation that will raise the standard of moral values from its pulpit and in its Sunday school classes.

12. *A church that helps people find the real reason for living.* The church my grandchildren attend must have a clearly defined mission for its existence. Too many churches apparently exist to support their own survival. I pray for the leaders of the church for the next generation that they will have a worldview that truly believes their community desperately needs Christ. I hope leaders will force the whole congregation to examine its role in society. Beyond that I wish for them a church that will be as interested in the spiritual health of the church as it is in the number who attend. That they will be involved in bringing Christ to their community. I pray the church they attend will enable them to live out

the wonderful message of Romans 12:11, "Not lagging in diligence, fervent in spirit, serving the Lord."

The church I dream about for the next generation should be a people of love and of enthusiasm for the gospel, but always vigilant. Like Nehemiah, they will stay alert to anything that might create disillusionment and apathy in the lives of the members of the congregation.

I will for the next generation a fellowship of saints who put on the whole armor of God so when Satan attacks, they do everything to stand firm. If the Lord tarries, I want my grandchildren to come to old age and look back on their parents, their children, and their grandchildren and be able to say about the church—the authentic family of God—that it is the greatest institution in the world and that they were proud to be a part of it.

That's the church I covet for the future generations of my family and for yours as well. My reasons for wanting such a church are explained in this poem penned by an anonymous author:

> *A builder builded a temple*
>   *He wrought with care and skill,*
> *Pillars and spires and arches*
>   *Were fashioned to meet his will.*
> *And men said when they saw its beauty,*
>   *"It shall never know decay.*
> *Great is thy skill, O Builder,*
>   *Thy fame shall endure for aye."*
>
> *A teacher builded a temple*
>   *She wrought with skill and care:—*
> *Forming each pillar with patience,*
>   *Laying each stone with prayer.*
> *None saw the unceasing effort;*

None knew of the marvelous plan;
For the temple the teacher builded
Was unseen by the eyes of man.

Gone is the builder's temple—
Crumbled into the dust.
Pillar and spires and arches
Food for consuming rust:
But the temple the teacher builded
Shall endure while the ages roll;—
For that beautiful unseen temple
Was a child's immortal soul.

About the Authors

H. B. London, Jr., is Vice President of Ministry Outreach/ Pastoral Ministries at Focus on the Family in Colorado Springs, Colorado. He is a fourth-generation minister and has pastored churches for thirty-one years, most recently a 3,200-member congregation in southern California. His assignments have taken him around the world in efforts related to revival, missions development, evangelism, pastoral training, and affirmation. At Focus on the Family he gives oversight to eight ministry departments, including its outreach to pastors and their families and church renewal. He has always been committed to the building and support of strong families through a loving and caring congregation of believers.

Neil B. Wiseman is Professor of Pastoral Development at Nazarene Bible College in Colorado Springs, Colorado. A veteran of more than twenty years in the pastorate, he has been involved in pastoral support ministry and theological education for another twenty years. Active beyond the classroom, Wiseman edits a quarterly magazine called *GROW,* serves as founder and director of the Small Church Institute, and is involved in several publishing projects. He also preaches in revivals, conferences, and camp meetings. Wiseman has edited or written twelve books—four with H. B. London, Jr., including *Is Your Pastor an Endangered Species?* and the bestselling *Pastors at Risk.*